SIDE *by* EACH

Side
by
Each

by

Willie

Snow

Ethridge

The
Vanguard Press
Inc.
New York

Library of Congress Catalogue Card Number: 73-83034
SBN 8149-0733-4
Designer: Ernst Reichl
Manufactured in the United States
of America

 SIDE *by* EACH

1

In 1963 the sad day came when my husband Mark, having reached the hoary age of sixty-seven (I married a man, you see, much too old for me), decided it was time for him to retire. For twenty-eight years he had been with the *Louisville Courier Journal, Louisville Times* and the Radio-TV station WHAS, serving for the first few years as general manager of the papers; then, publisher; and then, the last year, chairman of the board; and we had lived in the lovely village of Prospect, fourteen miles outside of Louisville. No amount of arguing—and I did argue—would budge him. He was tired of working, he said; he had been working since he was in high school—more than half a century—and he was ready to take it easy.

I was sympathetic with his line of reasoning but nevertheless I was dismayed. I wasn't ready to face up to the sobering fact we had reached the end of a very beautiful way of life. I was spoiled at being, through Mark's sensitive, important jobs, a vital part of the busy, exciting world, and I couldn't bear the thought of sitting on the side lines and watching others carry on.

For forty-two years I had been married to Mark, an exceedingly hard-working, energetic, ambitious, keen-minded, honest, strong-willed individual, and I simply couldn't picture myself living with a man who didn't go to a paper six mornings a week, not only ready, but eager, to do battle.

The more difficult the struggle, the more determined he was to solve it.

Frequently when I'm feeling kittenish, I say I married Mark when I was eleven in the Ogeechee swamps in South Georgia. He, on the other hand, declares he coaxed me, barefoot, when I was full grown, out of those swamps with a stick of peppermint candy. Both versions are slightly exaggerated. It is true I was born in Savannah in Chatham County, not far from the mouth of that clear, coffee-colored river, and I spent the first eight years of my youth in Guyton, Georgia, just three miles away from the Ogeechee's jungle-like banks; but I had been living in Macon eight years when Mark and I met.

(The place of my birth and of my early years, by the way, has nothing to do with my tacky name, Willie. My father was William Aaron Snow and when I, his first, was born, he insisted on naming me after him; he just couldn't wait. I was followed in due time by four brothers. The oldest was named Cubbedge, my mother's family name; the second, who died in infancy, Lewellyn; the third—you won't believe this—William Aaron, my father arguing that, after all, I, with the name of just Willie, wasn't really a proper namesake; and the fourth, James Edward.

(Being a girl named Willie is worse than being a boy named Sue. As I grew up, I regularly received letters from the secretary of the YMCA beginning, "Don't you ever expect to become a man?" and concluding with the suggestion that if I did I had better join the YMCA immediately. Enclosed with the letters were candid pictures of naked boys flexing their muscles and diving swanlike into the swimming pool. With those pornographic snapshots shoved periodically under my nose, I'll never understand how I grew up so normal.

~§ 2

(Conscientiously I'd reply I had no hopes of becoming a man—this was, of course, eons before Christine Jorgenson. For several months after dispatching my letter I wouldn't get any mail, for the YMCA was my only correspondent; then the YMCA would change secretaries—the turnover among this group must be terrific—and I would get another solicitation and a fresh batch of titillating snapshots.

(The absurdity of my being named Willie with a brother named William struck me hardest one day shortly after the publication of my first book, *As I Live and Breathe.* In the morning mail I received a letter from a resident of Guyton who wrote: "Dear Willie, I was so pleased to read in yesterday's paper you had written a book. You won't remember me, but I remember you quite well. On Sunday afternoons when I was a little girl, some member of my family, looking out the window, would call, 'Here comes Bill, Willie, William and the billygoat' and we would all rush to the front porch to see you go by.")

So, as I was saying, I was from Ogeechee swamp country; but all else in Mark's version of "getting to know" me is pure fiction. Prompted by curiosity, one of his more highly developed characteristics, he actually asked to meet me. At the time he was a young reporter on the *Macon Telegraph,* having come from Meridian, Mississippi, where he was born, via Columbus, Georgia, to Macon, and I was a senior in Lanier High School with more enthusiasm for basketball than for books. I played forward on the girls' team (we played by boys' rules; there was nothing sissy about us) and I put everything I had into the game except a small part of my heart dedicated to the *Telegraph's* sports editor, one George Sparks. And, fortunately for me, a goodly part of his heart was dedicated to me. Whenever Lanier's girls' team played, I starred in big headlines in the *Tele-*

3 ટ્ઠ

graph next morning. We could have been crushed, twenty-three to sixty-one, but still I starred.

This phenomenon had been going on for a good many months when, quite late in the season, either the end of April or the first of May, Mark, curious and confused, said to George, "I'd certainly like to meet that Willie Snow who stars no matter whether her team is clobbered ten to forty-five. She must be some girl."

"That she is," declared my faithful, guileless swain, and enthusiastically suggested that Mark accompany him the next Sunday night to the B.Y.P.U. (Baptist Young People's Union) where I would be.

That evening I "swished in," according to Mark, "in a dark blue taffeta dress" with my two brothers, Cubbedge and William, the three of us "giggling like mad."

After the B.Y.P.U. and the evening church service, Mark walked me home (dear George had to go back to the *Telegraph* to write his Monday column). We sat in the swing on the front porch where beams from the street light on the nearby corner thrust through the green swags of wisteria to scatter golden coins at our feet and we ate olive sandwiches and drank iced tea. Mark has always claimed it was the dark blue taffeta and the olive sandwiches, of which he is inordinately fond, that did him in. Anyway, that evening spelled the end of my starring career. George recognized my complete capitulation to Mark's charms even before I did, which was very quick work, for I knew almost immediately I was in love—terribly, terribly in love.

But what's more to the point is I never changed and I never turned loose. He was young, just twenty-one, which I figured was in my favor—he hadn't formed his taste yet. He did everything to shake me loose; he even joined the navy in the First World War, though he had never seen a body of water larger than Sowashee Creek in Mississippi; but I kept sending him come-back-to-me thought waves and, after three years, when the war was over, he came.

By then I was a junior in Wesleyan College in Macon and also a feature writer on the *Telegraph*. Determined to keep Mark's interest up when and if he came back, I had studied journalism during my freshman year and had, shortly thereafter, gone to work for the *Telegraph* in the afternoons for ten dollars a week.

In addition to part-time me, the *Telegraph* had four girl reporters, including the society editor (this was war!). When Mark isn't claiming he coaxed me out of the Ogee-chee swamps, he's bragging that he, as the newly ap-pointed city editor, in a drive to reduce the females on the staff, went far beyond the call of duty by marrying me. However, he didn't sacrifice himself until after I was grad-uated.

The first years after our marriage we were poor as the proverbial church mouse; Mark made only $50 a week—and he a city editor. It didn't worry me, however. Having never been accustomed to money (my father died when I was six-teen, leaving my mother with a very small income and my three brothers and me to put through college), I was com-pletely indifferent to our strapped financial situation. We had enough money for food, the necessary clothes, and a roof over our heads. So what?

In fact, we shared mother's roof. She moved upstairs in her fairly large, two-story wooden house and we occupied the downstairs, which consisted of a parlor; a dining room; an everyday sitting-breakfast room, which would now be called a "family room"; a kitchen; a bedroom; a sleeping porch, and a bath.

It was on a wide street that was then named Washington

Avenue but was changed long ago to Hardeman Avenue, along which a streetcar clanged all day and far into the night. On the plush side it faced the campus of Wesleyan, a lush green area with huge old magnolias and oaks, many of them draped with wisteria; but it backed on an alley of mustard-colored shanties teeming with Negroes, for our house, like hundreds of others in Macon, was in a block that put up a good front while covering a decaying behind.

One year and one month from our wedding day we had our first-born, Mary Snow, whom we nicknamed Shug. When she was still an infant in a basket we moved to New York so Mark could have what he described as "metropolitan experience." For two busy, enlightening years he worked as a reporter on the old *Sun* and did weekly features for the *Atlanta Journal Sunday Magazine* and I wrote articles for *Good Housekeeping* magazine and, with Mark's help, produced Mark Foster Jr., whom we called Bubber.

In 1925 we returned to Macon, had another child whom we named Georgia and whom, surprisingly, we called Georgia, and Mark became associate and managing editor of the *Telegraph* and of the afternoon paper, the *News,* which the *Telegraph* had recently bought. He not only oversaw the publication of these two papers, but wrote practically two columns of editorials daily and edited all the columns and letters for the *Telegraph.* He went to work at ten o'clock every morning, except Sunday, when he didn't go until late afternoon, and came home between two and three o'clock in the morning. Naturally, the children scarcely knew him. Once when I was driving them down Cherry Street, Macon's main drag, Shug, on glimpsing a man somewhat similar in size to Mark, yelled excitedly, "Muh-mum, is that my daddy?"

This busy, happy Georgia phase of our lives was shot sky

high in early 1933 by a telegram to Mark from the Carl Schurz Foundation, announcing a sufficient amount of German marks had been deposited in a bank in Berlin so that he and I could spend six months traveling in Middle Europe. Mark had applied several months before for a fellowship from this foundation on the grounds that he would like to study the "ramifications of the Versailles Treaty" that were causing so much debate and bitterness in Germany, Poland, and Czechoslovakia. The news that enough money had been alloted for me to accompany him came as a big and delightful surprise.

Blithely leaving the three children with my mother, who never muttered a complaining word, one bitter February morning we boarded our ship, the *Stuttgart* of the North German Lloyd Line, in New York and, after eleven days, landed in Bremen on March 6, the day after Hitler had come to power. On Sunday evening, while still on the ship, we had heard that Hitler's party, in conjunction with the Nationalist Party of Von Hindenburg and Von Papen, had obtained a slight majority in that day's election and that the little-known Bavarian paperhanger was now the country's *Führer.*

That day of our arrival was not only a significant date in the history of Germany, but also in the history of the United States. On March 4, just the day before the Hitler victory, Franklin Roosevelt had been inaugurated President, and on that Monday he had declared the bank moratorium, which reached all across the Atlantic to tag us. When Mark first tried to exchange some American money for German marks, he was told it was impossible, as there was no quotation of its worth.

For the next 180 days we witnessed at close hand the many machinations of the Nazi revolution. We attended

Hitler rallies; we were at Potsdam for Hitler's "crowning"; we followed parades; we crashed Nazi lines picketing Jewish-owned stores; we studied Hitler from just a few feet away (I could have dropped a brick on him and I will never forgive myself that I didn't) at the Munich Opera House as he drank in the music of *Tristan und Isolde;* we. . . . Oh, we had the most stirring and the most disturbing six months.

When we returned to the States, Mark was without a job. While he was away, the *Telegraph* had turned its back on the liberal causes for which he had so zealously fought, including the presidency of Mr. Roosevelt, and, sick at heart, he had resigned. After looking about for a few uneasy weeks, he went with the Washington Bureau of the Associated Press to write what is now called news analysis, but after a very short while resigned to work for Mr. Eugene Meyer on the *Washington Post* as associate editor, which meant, of course, that the children and I moved to Washington too. Then, after eighteen months on that exciting, challenging paper, he left to become publisher of the *Richmond* (Va.) *Dispatch;* and then, after seventeen months, he resigned once again to accept the offer from Ambassador Robert Worth Bingham and his son Barry to come to Louisville.

Mark's years there had been exceedingly full and rewarding. In addition to his newspaper and radio-TV responsibilities, he had served as the first president of the National Association of Broadcasters, which he had helped reorganize; he had been chairman of the Fair Employment Practice Committee, set up by President Roosevelt just before World War II to get full employment of every able-bodied man, particularly of Negroes and members of other minority groups; he had chaired from 1948 through 1951 the Advisory Commission on Information, which oversaw the Voice of America and Films Abroad; he had served as a member of the President's Farm Tenancy Committee, which sponsored and pushed through the Bankhead Bill, and he had gone on three extensive missions for the United States Government. First, in 1945, he was sent by Secretary of State James Byrnes to Bulgaria, Rumania, and Russia to find out if it was true that the Soviet forces, which had moved into the Balkans, were violating the Yalta Agreement that called for Bulgaria and Rumania to have free elections. Second, in 1947, he headed the American Delegation of the Balkan Commission, to investigate Greek border disorders; and third, in 1949, he headed the American Delegation of the Palestine Commission, newly created to bring about, if possible, a permanent peace to Israel and the Arab world. I accompanied him on these last two missions and wrote my experiences in the books *It's Greek to Me* and *Going to Jerusalem.*

Besides these activities and many, many others, he had sired our fourth child, William Davidson Ethridge, whom we called, during his young years, Mr. Big. Then, as the years rolled on and on, we had married off all four of the children and had accumulated twelve grandchildren. Our oldest, Shug, had married Frank J. Abbott Jr., nicknamed, naturally, Bud, who had migrated to Louisville from New Hampshire and they had three children: Mark, Sefton, and Georgia Snow. Our second-born, Bubber, had married Margaret, called Peg, Furbee of Fairmont, West Virginia, and they had four: Mark III, Russell, Peggy, and Mary Davidson. Our third, Georgia, had married Marc Schneider of Louisville and they had four: David, Jenny, Georgia Cubbedge, and Mary Howell. The youngest, David, had married Eleanor Taft of Louisville and so far they had only one offspring, David Jr.

Now, after all these exceedingly happy and eventful years, we were to go into retirement. At least Mark was going into retirement and where Mark went I was sure to go. Everything—well, practically everything—would be different. Very different. Mark insisted not only on retiring, but retiring a considerable distance from Louisville where he wouldn't be tempted to look over the shoulders of those who filled his shoes and give them unwanted advice. He needed to be so far away that by the time the papers reached him it would be too late for him to call up and say what was wrong with them—and, of course, though he didn't come right out and say so, there would be plenty wrong with them. He must cut himself completely loose, he argued; he must not look back unless he was called upon in some crisis.

So the question was—where to retire? Some people I know retire where they have no children and grandchildren. They move hundreds of miles away and set themselves down among total strangers. To see their precious loved ones they have to travel days and nights or else the loved ones have to travel days and nights and visit them for one or two exhausting weeks.

And these misguided people not only settle where they have no children and grandchildren, but frequently settle among strangers their own age or even older. It is difficult enough to live with one old person, but to be surrounded by ancients is my idea of slow death. I wanted to be around the young just as much as the young would allow me to be. I wanted to share their interests, their dancing partners, their books, their ambitions. Old people at best have a tendency to sit on their withered behinds and reminisce on what has been. I longed to look forward, to have new, fresh, exciting experiences. Just because one has reached sixty-five is no reason to withdraw from the go-go people and bury oneself among the faltering and shuffling. And for once, thank goodness, Mark agreed with me, though, of course, I let him think I was agreeing with him.

It would have been best if we could have retired where all the children and grandchildren were; but since they lived in different places, that was impossible. The Abbotts live in Sanford, North Carolina; the Mark Ethridge Jrs. in Akron; the Schneiders in Pittsburgh, and the David Ethridges in Chapel Hill, North Carolina. So North Carolina seemed the obvious place. With two sets of children and grandchildren there and the climate much more congenial to our southern blood than that of Akron and Pittsburgh, it won hands down.

However, neither Mark nor I wanted to be right on the doorsteps of our North Carolina progeny. We didn't want their friends to feel obliged to have us to their parties because we were underfoot when our own children were invited. Also, we didn't want to be too accessible for baby-sitting. It was fine, we felt, to be asked to move in with grandchildren when their parents went off for holidays (we knew they weren't sufficiently well-heeled to go off often); but we didn't care for the idea of babies being dumped on us for long evenings while mamas and papas disappeared into the wild blue yonder or, even worse, bundle ourselves up and sit in strange chairs under insufficient lights, struggling to keep our old eyes open until the wee hours when the parents would return. Though we considered ourselves still youthful enough to associate with the young, we liked to be able to crawl into bed when weariness overtook us, even at seven o'clock, and watch television or read.

Ten or twenty miles away from both Carolina families would be about right, we decided, and in the country, the real country. For the last twenty-eight years we had lived

11 ૨૦

in the country and loved it, so why, just because we must retire, should we change our way of living and move into an apartment in a town or city? Why should we coop ourselves up? We had both worked hard all our lives to be financially able to spend our old age in the manner to which we had grown accustomed. Why pull into a shell like a turtle? Why cut out a single interest unless it was obligatory? Mark was giving up the great thrill and responsibility of running two newspapers and we were both giving up our close association with many dearly beloved friends; so why give up anything more?

"What will you do if you become ill or incapacitated?" friends asked us.

"We will face that when the time comes," we answered.

And we meant it. Why admit before it was necessary that we might need doctors? Why live in fear? There were still telephones and cars.

We set our hearts on building a house in the woods and continuing our lives as normally as possible. We, especially I, loved the country. I adored digging in the ground, planting, pruning, raking, fertilizing, dreaming. . . . And though Mark had shown no inclination in any of these directions, I had big hopes that he might. With time on his hands, why shouldn't he become enthusiastic about growing things? I knew of a good many men who, after they retired, had become camellia growers and holly fanciers and azalea specialists. Surely as the months rolled by, Mark would take up some outdoor hobby other than golf. For the first time in our lives we would know the pleasure of working side by each—and that would be something.

2

I went out from Sanford, North Carolina, in late March, five months before Mark was to retire, to look for a piece of land on which to build the house. I was baby-sitting at the time with my nine-year-old grandson Mark Abbott, while Bud and Shug were at an eye, nose, and throat clinic in Durham to have out the tonsils of the two younger children, Sefton and Georgia Snow. Having the Sunday afternoon free (I can't remember now what I did with Mark A.), I called up a real-estate man and asked him if he could show me some wooded acreage with water—preferably a river— on it. For a couple of hours he drove me around the suburbs of Sanford where small, artificial ponds had been scooped out and where there were all shapes and sizes of lots for sale; but none of them appealed to me.

"I'm looking for land with lots of trees and running water," I kept telling him. "I've always wanted a house with a river view. My one regret about our home in Kentucky was I couldn't see the Ohio River except when all the leaves were off the trees and I climbed up on the roof. I'd really like a hilltop with a river at the bottom of it."

The realtor shook his head in bafflement. Sanford is on the very eastern edge of the section of North Carolina called the Piedmont. Though the land rolls gently in some areas, it is mostly flat, especially south of Sanford, where it quickly turns sandy as it approaches those nearby elegant golf resorts of Southern Pines and Pinehurst.

Finally, after showing me more suburban lots and receiving no affirmative response from me, the realtor said he did know of some land with a small river, called Rocky, ten miles from Sanford, on the highway to Chapel Hill and Durham, that the owner had just put on the market; but he feared it was too far in the country for me.

"Not at all," I assured him. "I've been living in the country fourteen miles from Louisville for twenty-eight years and loving it."

"Okay, if you're sure you don't mind the distance," he agreed, but with no enthusiasm. It was plain to see he thought I was wasting his Sunday afternoon.

On reaching the property, we turned to the left on a narrow, rutty clay road that had been cut about ten years before when the woods had been timbered. Bumping along for approximately a quarter of a mile, we came to a small, flat, partially cleared area, parked the car, and got out. Tall, slender pines, oaks, maples, dogwood, hollies, hickories, and masses of sumac and blackberry briars encircled us; but ten feet or so away from where we stood, on the west side, the land started plunging downward. At the foot of the incline, 192 feet below us, so the real-estate salesman told me, was Rocky River. I couldn't see it, though; the trees and underbrush were much too thick and the drop too precipitous. However, I could hear it gurgling. I got excited. I left the real-estate man and fought my way for fifteen or so yards down the slope until I reached a stump. With the help of an overhanging limb, I managed to climb atop of it. Then, miracle of miracles, I saw to my right a calm, graceful curve of water, the deep green of olives, and, directly below me, between the boles and branches of trees, I glimpsed scraps of white, lacy underwear ruffles as the river hop-skipped over helter-skelter lines of cream-colored rocks. On the other side of the stream, thickly wooded banks rolled away to far distant hills that merged eventually into the clear blue sky.

I was enchanted. I was beside myself with joy. It was the kind of view I had dreamed of all my life. And suddenly it hit me like a muchly needed summer shower that retirement couldn't be as bad as I had feared if I could feel such a thrill on finding so beautiful a place where Mark and I might settle. My soaring spirits didn't fit the picture of a finished-off, end-of-the-road character. This new life for Mark and me could be full of "exciting outlets and pulsing channels."

The only mistake I made was to tell the real-estate man, who had struggled down the bluff to stand beside me, how mad I was about the view. Then quite cockily he told me that if I wanted the property, I had better close the deal immediately. He said the owner wasn't at all happy about selling, but he had agreed on the spur of the moment to sell it if he could get his price.

"How many acres are there?" I inquired, coming back to earth.

"Three hundred."

I gasped.

Seeing my shock, he said that though the owner wanted to sell all three hundred, he would sell fifty for half the price he was asking for the three hundred. I, of course, wanted the three hundred. I felt it was a crime to pass up three hundred acres when they would cost only twice as much as fifty. It really didn't make sense. Then I remembered Mark still slaving back in Louisville. What would he think if I agreed to buy three hundred acres of wild woods? The answer came loud and clear. He would think I had lost my feeble mind. Just as plainly as if he were present, I could hear him asking scathingly what would we do with three hundred acres of land. And when I told him we would grow Christmas trees—this brilliant idea had come to me instantly—and call the land a farm and take it off the income tax, I could hear him ask even more scathingly who would take care of them. Positively, not he.

So reluctantly I told the real-estate man I was afraid the three hundred acres were out of the question, but I was practically sure we would take fifty. However, I couldn't be absolutely sure until Mark saw them, for after all he was going to have to pay for them.

"Okay," he said, "but you and Mr. Ethridge better make up your minds fast before the owner changes his."

The minute I got back to Shug's and Bud's house I telephoned Mark to come immediately. He, not having seen the vision I had seen, said he could not get away until the coming weekend. After all, he still had a job for which I should be grateful. "Keep your shirt on," he advised me elegantly. "Don't do anything rash."

The next morning I, still soaring like a bird, went to the hospital in Durham to sit with Shug and the two tonsilectomy patients while Bud returned to Sanford and the radio station he and Shug owned. In spite of Georgia and Sefton screaming their heads off and spitting blobs of blood (the nurse on duty, tch-tching, said Shug had made a terrible mistake having their tonsils out when the moon was in the head instead of the feet), I tried to describe the land to Shug. But how could I picture the breathtaking steepness and jungle-like wildness of the slope plunging from that little cleared plateau at the summit to the river's edge, and the river itself, one section above the bend a seemingly still spread of shining emerald and the section below the bend a team of rushing, white-clad tackles battering a blocking line of boulders? Shug kept shaking her head. She simply couldn't believe I had found this heaven so close to Sanford.

"You just wait and see," I crowed. "You just wait and see."

She didn't have long to wait. The very next morning, when Sefton and Georgia were dismissed, we drove straight to the site and, leaving the still-suffering and wailing "amputees" in the car, we breast-stroked our way to the stump. Immediately Shug realized I hadn't exaggerated one whit the beauty of the spot. Ecstatic as I, she insisted Mark and I must have it. She would call her father the first second she could get to a phone and tell him to come with all speed; he must not let anything detain him.

Mark did come on the weekend as he had promised; but not alone. He brought our Prospect neighbor, Morton Boyd, who was the president of the Commonwealth Life Insurance and in that role was familiar with the worth of land, and his wife Pauline. As Mark confided to me later, he had urged Morton to tell me not to buy the land; that the price was too steep; that the woods had been timbered of its best trees; that it was too remote from the nearest town, which, as we had learned, was not Sanford, but Pittsboro, six and a half miles to the east. However, when Morton saw it, he advised us to buy it if it had a supply of good drinking water. "You should never buy land," said he, "without first finding out if you can get water."

"I'm afraid there won't be time to find that out in this case," spoke up the real-estate man. "The deal will have to be closed by Monday and, as you know, this is Saturday. The owner has had a change of heart and doesn't want to sell the land at all. He has told me he will sell it to you, Mr. Ethridge, since I did assure Mrs. Ethridge it was for

17 ⟨⟨⟩

sale, but unless you close the deal immediately, he is taking it off the market. He wants to build on it himself."

I wrung my hands and pulled my hair. "Oh, Mark, we must buy it," I pleaded. "We simply must buy it."

"But what are going to do about the water?" Mark demanded.

"I don't care about water. We can drink the water out of the river, if necessary."

So we bought the fifty acres by Monday noon. We would have bought them that very hour, except the courthouse was closed.

And from that day on we were as proud possessors as any peasants upon whom a generous shah had bestowed some of his ancestral inheritance. We couldn't stay away from our land. We made innumerable visits to Sanford, ostensibly to see Shug, Bud, and the grandchildren; but in truth they were made so we could sit for a few hours on our domain.

Our plan to move to North Carolina as soon as Mark retired that fall from the *Courier Journal* and *Times* was upset by the untimely death of our close friend Alicia Patterson Guggenheim, editor of that miraculously successful Long Island paper, *Newsday*, and the need of her husband Harry for someone to take her place until he could find a permanent editor. Harry was in real distress. He had had no experience on the editorial side of the paper; his role had been entirely in the business end. He needed an experienced newspaperman—not with the genius of Alicia (that couldn't be duplicated)—who could by his own knowledge, ability, and tact take hold with a tight rein and drive *Newsday's* amazingly diverse, temperamental, and talented staff. Harry also wanted—or at least he thought he wanted—an older hand to teach and to counsel Alicia's nephew, Joe Albright, on how to run a newspaper so that someday he could take over as publisher. This need of Harry's appealed to Mark very much. Joe was smart (how else could he be with Patterson blood?) and exceedingly personable. Training him would give Mark great satisfaction. For the last few years he had worked with Mary and Barry Bingham's brilliant eldest son Worth, to fit him, when his father retired, to head the *Courier Journal* and *Times* and had relished every hour of it. So he agreed to go to *Newsday* as editor for two years, no more, and we moved to Garden City, Long Island.

When the two-year stint was up, we took an apartment in Chapel Hill to wait out the building of the house. Chapel Hill was more convenient than Sanford, for Mark had taken on another job—he was conducting weekly three-hour seminars in the journalism department of the University of North Carolina.

We took every friend who came to visit us in Chapel Hill to Rocky River to see the land and to have a picnic on the partly cleared area at the top of the bluff. Indeed, we talked so much about the land and invited so many people to see the land (after all, we couldn't invite them to see the house when there wasn't any house) that the name 'The Land' stuck permanently.

All our friends, except one, were exceedingly generous in their praise. No doubt they were afraid not to be. "Look at the river!" I'd command as soon as I arrived with a virgin viewer at the look-out stump. "Look how gracefully the limbs of the trees hang over the water! . . . Look at the reflection of the trees; every leaf is distinct! . . . Look how the pines soar against the sky! . . . Look how you can see forever and ever! . . . Look! Look! Look!" The one unappreciative visitor was Ellen Bryan, the wife of Wright, who was then the vice-president of Clemson University in Clemson, South Carolina. After I had screamed "Look!" until my throat was sore, she said in the most disgustingly blasé manner, "It's all right if you want to live in the bushes." And she from Clemson, mind you!

On every trip, especially with the coming of spring, I'd discover new, undreamed-of, glorious surprises. Having bought the land in late March before the trees came into leaf and bloom, I never dreamed the woods simply teemed with dogwood in April, when their dazzling white petals floated beneath the pines and other tall trees as thickly as foam over spent ocean breakers, nor with sourwood, their strings of pale yellow bells dangling as daintily as lilies of the valley from the tips of their crimson limbs.

One May day, exploring along the riverbank a goodly distance to the south of the small cleared area, I floundered into a jungle—yes, a real jungle—of mountain laurel bursting like Roman candles in huge, soft pink flowers. It was a glorious shock. Though laurel abounds in the mountains of North Carolina, it is practically unknown in this part of the state. The river had evidently washed the seed down from much higher ground. Among the laurel grows what I in my Georgia days had called "grancy greybeard," but what the wild-flower books call "fringe tree." By whatever name, it is enchanting in the spring, draped as it is like properly decorated Christmas trees with the silver icicles of its dripping, silken flowers. Also in this laurel jungle are hollies, as well as cedars, pines, wild azaleas, dogwood, maples, sassafras, shad bushes, and innumerable other choice items.

The only drawback to this paradise when I first found it was a carpet, three or four feet deep, of dead rubbish that had been swept in spring after spring when Rocky flooded. Much of the rubbish was composed of short, brittle sections of cane that appeared as firm as woven chair bottoms, but that, when I tried to walk across them, allowed my feet and legs to sink down and down and down, throwing me on my surprised but still ecstatic face.

Another day, directly in front of what at that moment I thought would be the ideal location for the house, I discovered in just one big, vigorous clump of greenery two hollies, three dogwoods, three wild azaleas, two mountain laurels, and a towering, V-pronged oak. In one clump! Still another day I found a gently rolling hilltop glistening with practically nothing but hollies. There are at least a half-hundred there, many of their gray trunks hoary with age. One prize specimen has five big trunks, springing, so it seems, from one root. Almost too good to be true, two of the silvery trunks lean far over a small stream bed that winds about the foot of the hill.

And close by, just a glance below the main mass of hollies, are countless hawthorns, during their flowering season white and airy as a bride's veil. The first spring I saw them spreading their snowy drifts over the land I began dreaming of a May wedding there of my Sanford granddaughter, Georgia.

A continuous fountain of ferns leaps up from the rocky banks of a stream bed, unfortunately frequently dry, that runs in the crevice of a long ravine extending from a cluster of cedars, entwined with yellow jasmine, near the highway, all the way to the river. In late January and early February, the tiny, shy blue blooms of hepatica polka-dot the brown, pine-needle sides of this baby chasm; a little later in the year and much nearer the river, dogtooth violets bare their green-gold flowers above thick carpets of tawny-spotted, leather-thick leaves; many little clumps of blue-eyed christata sing out from nests of gnarled roots; and . . . . oh, I could go on and on and on.

Once, when I caught myself raving lyrically to a group of

visitors about the natural, wild beauty of the land, I said, to excuse myself, "I can brag about it because I didn't have anything to do with it; God gave it to me." At which Mark, standing by, brooding over the mortgage, exploded, "To hell He did!"

3

All our fifty acres were so beautiful, I couldn't make up my mind where to build the house. For days, for weeks, even for months I'd thrash my way along the brow of the bluff, peering through the brush and tree boles at the river. Did I want most a view of the placid water curving around the bend? Or did I prefer a more extensive view of the rapids buffeting the impeding rocks?

Some days I'd lean to more still water; other days I'd lean to more white water. Listening on one occasion to my hemming and hawing, Bud advised, "Why don't you put the house like a railroad train on tracks? Then you can move it up and down with the changing of your mind."

Not only did I have to consider the different views, but the trees and shrubs on the bluff. There were two large white oaks about twenty feet apart just where the level land began to fall off to the river that I could picture framing the front door if the house were built just a little to the rear of them. On the other hand, if the house were put there, a patch of wild azaleas and a couple of hollies would have to be sacrificed.

A hundred feet or more to the left of this spot, the ground was almost barren except for a wilderness of little pines, sumac, honeysuckle vines, and blackberry briars; but the house on that site wouldn't command so wide a view of the river beyond the bend and the distant hills.

Still farther to the left, the bluff ran out to a point almost perpendicularly above the river, with magnificent shaggy-bark hickories towering over it and the land on one side dropping dramatically away to the fern-filled ravine; but if we built there, the logging road, which we were counting on converting into a road to the house, would have to be extended considerably and that would be quite expensive.

What a problem! I couldn't sleep at night for trying to decide this vital question: where to put the house.

As for the house itself, I knew exactly the kind I wanted: a Japanese house. Mark and I had been to Japan in the summer of 1963 and I had fallen head over heels in love with those sliding doors and windows, those movable screens and low, picturesque roofs. Mark, though, put his foot down. He argued that if we had to sell the house someday, there would be too limited a market for there were so few Japanese in North Carolina.

Seeing he had a point there, I happily settled for a considerably altered version of a house that had belonged to our friends, the Harold Johnsons, back in Kentucky, a dozen miles or so from Prospect. The Johnson house had a large, enclosed brick-paved "dogtrot," with two extensive wings; indeed, one was so extensive it rambled away to include a library, two dining rooms—one for the master and mistress of the house and one for the servants—a kitchen, storerooms, servants' quarters, garages, and other "accoutrements" of the rich.

In our cut-down version, the dogtrot, which the Johnsons used as a garden room with countless pots of geraniums, tea olives, begonias, dwarf lemon trees and what-have-you, would be our living room and the wings on either side would have three main rooms with such extras as closets, baths, laundry niches, porch, and deck. To be more explicit, on one side of the living room would be a combined library-dining room, an open deck, a screened-in porch, a kitchen, a laundry, and a maid's room (what mad dreams I had in those days) and bath; and on the other side of the living room would be the master bedroom with a dressing room each for Mark and me, and a bath, and two guest rooms and baths.

Though we knew what we wanted, we needed an architect to collapse a sixteen- or seventeen-room mansion into an eight-room cottage and retain the charm of the original. Neither Mark nor I knew the name of an architect in North Carolina, but fortunately Shug knew one, the late Ed Lowenstein of Greensboro, whom she recommended highly, for he had married the first cousin of a girl who was at Duke University with her in the dim past. Shug had even been to his very exciting, modern home that among other last-word features had a fireplace without a chimney, set in a wall of glass. The fireplace was fantastic, she said, "absolutely fantastic," and Mark and I must have one just like it. I could scarcely wait.

While Mark and I were still living on Long Island, Shug and I drove to Greensboro to see if Ed would take the job (oh, stars, does one say an architect "takes a job"? I'm always saying we "rented a yacht"—well, not quite always, we rented one only once; but the correct word, as I've been told repeatedly, is "chartered." I certainly don't want to downgrade what one does with an architect. Maybe I should say we went to Greensboro to inquire if he would accept the assignment).

"Have you some idea of the kind of house you want?" asked Ed, who was exceedingly handsome in a big, rugged way.

"Oh, yes, I know exactly."

25 ᘒ

"What type is it?"

"Type?" I questioned.

"Yes. Is it Colonial? Modern? Temporary? Spanish? Salt-box?"

"Oh, I don't know what type. I just know how I want it to look and how many rooms it needs to have."

"Fine. Why don't you draw it off for me?" He shoved a large sheet of drafting paper and a pencil across the desk to me.

"I'm not much at drawing," I said quite truthfully, "but maybe I can give you a general idea."

"That will do fine."

Slowly I drew a plan that looked something like this:

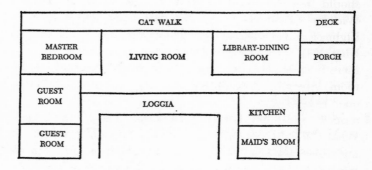

As you see, I didn't attempt to draw in bathrooms, dressing rooms, laundry, or doors and windows.

"Early Federal," Ed exclaimed when I had finished. "That's splendid. It is ideally suited to this section of the United States. The early settlers in North Carolina frequently built log houses with dogtrots in the middle."

I was pleased as a new mother. I had no idea I had chosen an Early Federal style, but now that I'd heard of it, I liked it immensely. It sounded so historic.

The next question was what kind of material we intended to use. "Wood," I answered, but that wasn't sufficient for Ed. California redwood? Cedar? Cypress? Japanese mahogany? At least I believe Ed mentioned Japanese mahogany. I know he mentioned some kind of mahogany because I said I thought it would be too dark and he said it came in light shades.

This was my introduction to the hundreds, nay thousands, of unthought-of-before, headache-producing, unfathomable, unanswerable questions that architects think up to throw at their innocent, simple-minded clients. For interminable weeks they went on. Asbestos shingles or cedar shakes? Windows with or without blinds? If with blinds, should they open and shut or should they be stationary? Wide or narrow floor boards? Oak, pine, maple, gum . . . ? Light or dark finish? What color brick for the loggia? (For what?) In what design should the brick be laid? Should there be a door between the living room and library-dining room? And if a door, should it be a single- or double-hung one? How wide the hall? Marble, tile, or vinyl for the bathroom floors? Faucets—porcelain, brass, gold-plated, nickel? What color bathtubs, toilets, washbasins? How high the living-room ceiling? Should it be beamed, plastered, wallpapered? How many cabinets in the kitchen? What height? What depth? What width? What length? What walls? How about the library-dining room? Just how big did it need to be? Should the bookcases extend from the floor to the ceiling or should there be cupboards beneath them? If cupboards, how many and how big? Were the fireplaces to be faced with marble, brick, tile? Should the fireplace be "manteled" or "mantelless"? What dimensions for the living room, the library-dining room, the kitchen, the guest rooms, the master bedroom, the master bedroom bath? (I must have been thinking of midgets when I suggested the size for this cleansing and purifying necessity, for it ended up as big as a low-priced station wagon. If I need to get by Mark while he is shaving at the washbasin, I have to walk in the bathtub to reach the chest above the toilet.) Which rooms were to be papered? Which plastered and, if plastered, how plastered—flat or shiny? What color—eggshell, oyster, white, or cream? How about the brass locks and knobs for the doors? How wide should the gallery, the loggia, and the catwalk be? Should the catwalk extend across the full length of the house? And on and on, ad infinitum.

Ed and I exchanged voluminous letters, but they weren't sufficient. Every month or so I traveled to Sanford and met Ed at The Land or on the porch of a shabby, rambling hotel in Siler City, which was closer to Greensboro than The Land, to roll the blueprints out on the floor, and discuss, discuss, discuss. Then Mark and I moved to Chapel Hill and the consultations became more frequent.

At long last all the questions were answered to the best of Mark's and my ability, the plans completed, a contractor, Jack Watson of Sanford, engaged, the bids let out, returned, and studied in horrified disbelief. No house of eight rooms— seven, really (I had been counting the cubbyhole of a laundry and flower-arranging nook to make it sound more important)—could possibly cost the outrageous sum those estimates added up to. Who did "they" think Mark was? Didn't they understand Mark had always been a salaried man who shared his every nickel with Uncle Sam?

For days we fumed; then cooled down sufficiently to do some cutting down. We lopped off two small appendages we had tacked on to Mark's and my bedroom that were to have been his-and-her studies. Learning their cost, we could see we would have to study twenty-three hours and forty-five minutes out of every twenty-four to make them self-supporting, as it were. And we settled for perfectly plain cabinets in the kitchen—no fancy trim, regular-sized doors that mills carry already made up, and no moldings.

With these last details settled, we were ready to break ground. What exhilarating days! What divinely happy, sleepless nights; there was much too much to think about to spend time sleeping. Truly, building a house is the greatest adventure. There is nothing I have ever experienced that so sparks the mind, tingles the blood, and lifts the spirit. It is the most satisfactory therapy; the heart ceases completely to ache for past scenes and old friends. In fact, it is all but impossible even to recall past scenes and old friends. I recommend building, if there is any money available, to everyone who retires and moves to a strange place. No matter whether it is just a very small, simple house. The task of creating a home shoves all regrets aside and fills every day with fresh, shiny, brand-new expectations.

Near the beginning of the year 1966, Ed, Jack, the bricklayers, the carpenters, Mark, and I were ready for the ground-breaking. We held no celebration then; we were too overwhelmed with a sense of anticipation and adventure; but on April 22, when the sturdy brick wall that ran the full length of the underpinnings of the house to give it support was completed, Shug, Bud, Eleanor, and David gave a big surprise party "on the grounds" for Mark. Not only was this "great" wall finished but it was Mark's seventieth birthday.

And when I say it was a "surprise" party, I'm being even more factual than I usually am. In spite of his keen nose for news, Mark never once suspected that a party was in the cards. We were visiting Shug and Bud in Sanford for what he thought was to be a simple family dinner with, perhaps, a coconut cake (his very favorite) and candles, and he never changed this notion even when his sister Ruth and her husband Ross Silkett arrived from Washington and our beloved friends, Barbara and John Welburn Brown, arrived from Louisville. The Silketts said they were on their way home from Florida and the Browns said they were returning from a month in Jamaica and all four insisted they had just dropped by en route.

In fact, Mark's innocence was so real that on the morning of the birthday he said to me, "I think we ought to get Ruth and Ross and Barbara and John out of Shug's hair. She's having all of us for dinner tonight and that's all she should have to do. Why don't you go to town and buy some sandwiches, potato chips, dill pickles, and things like that so we six can go to The Land and have a picnic?" And with that he forked over a twenty-dollar bill.

So I went to town and bought a little food and then, around noon, I picked up him, the Silketts, and the Browns and we drove to The Land. On reaching the entrance Mark saw David tacking a sign with the name "Ethridge" painted in red on a tree trunk and grew considerably agitated. "What's David doing that for?" he demanded of me. "We don't want people to know we are building a house back in these woods."

Not until we arrived at the wall and he saw to the right of it a fine gathering of people and gaily covered tables heaped with drinks and glasses and food and plates did the truth dawn upon him.

It was in my opinion the very happiest of parties. With so much to celebrate, everyone threw himself and herself into a festive mood. There were amusing presents—one friend, Clawson Williams Jr., who had just been made head of the board of ABC, presented Mark with a "brown bag" with a Coca Cola in it, and Margaret Rose and Terry Sanford brought him a wise old porcelain owl; and there was considerable consumption of both liquid and solid refreshments, especially of fried chicken. The most beautiful grand dame of Chapel Hill, Memory Lester, kept tossing bones over her shoulder while solemnly assuring us she was planting chickens so we would never go hungry.

And there was singing! And oh, such singing with a friend of David's from Durham, Eli Evans, playing the guitar and Mark doing the leading. There's nothing in the world Mark would rather do than sing. Yet, tragic to relate, he has no voice whatever. Still, that gives him staying power. Using, as he does, only one note, he never, never tires. Also, on the plus side, is his total recall of all the words of practically every old familiar song, including the Baptist and Methodist hymns, and these he "lines out" for his choruses between notes. He even "lines out" all the words of *The Star-Spangled Banner* and all the innumerable verses of *The Battle Hymn of the Republic*, his true love.

However, building the house wasn't all music and roses.

I drove every day, rain or shine, to see the progress being made, taking Mark with me when he wasn't too busy with his seminars at the University. Usually I was enchanted at what was happening, even if nothing more had been accomplished than the excavation of the basement; but as the weeks passed and the house began to take shape, I found now and then something not entirely to my liking.

One morning I arrived to discover the first rough boards of the floor had been laid. Thrilled, I tripped over piles of brick, laths, and dirt and stepped through the yawning hole that would be the front door. I couldn't wait to see how the river actually looked from the elevation of the house, especially as one entered; but to my disappointment, there was no view of the river from the front door or even from the wide hall that ran the length of the house and that Ed called the gallery. The floor projected so far over the bluff that it cut off completely any sight of the water. I could see only the feathery, new-leafed limbs of the oaks and maples and the the dark green needles of pines that sprang skyward from the fast-descending slope. I moved from the hall into the living room where I had anticipated entertaining my entranced guests and spending many of my leisure hours. Still no glimpse of the river, except across the library-dining room floor where I could see in the distance the clean, un-wrinkled, forest-green sheet above the footboard of the rapids. But where were the rapids? In a swoop I reached the outer boundary of the living room, where the windows and doors to the catwalk would someday be. Thank God, the rapids were still there, furiously tossing their white, curly manes as they jumped the rocky barriers.

I needn't go all the way to the imagined windows to see the river, Jack ventured in his timid, small voice. Maybe I would be able to see it from a little farther back in the room, sitting down. At this suggestion, George, Jack's brother and right-hand man, who had been standing by, produced a carpenter's bench and placed it a foot or two back from the windows and I sat down. Then he and Jack and the other workmen, who had abandoned hammering nails into boards to watch this performance, waited anxiously for the out-come. Yes, I could still see the river. They beamed; I beamed. George moved the bench back a few feet and I sat down again. Ah, yes, I could still see the river. This routine was repeated again and then again until the bench and I reached the middle of the room and I announced, "No more river. Only trees."

By then the disappointment had eased. I would make a habit of sitting near the windows and let those crass people who weren't crazy about water sit to the rear of the room.

As Jack, George, and I were finishing this experiment, a young assistant of Ed's, who came every week from Greensboro to check on the progress of the work, arrived and, hearing of my surprise at not being able to have a river view from all parts of the house, explained why it was an impossibility unless the whole house had been cantilevered over the bluff and windows let into the floor. As the house was planned, only the catwalk was cantilevered; the main section was laid over a basement, and the two wings extending out from the main section were almost flat on the ground.

I accepted readily the assistant's explanation; but I wasn't always so easily mollified. One day, many weeks later, we came close to the parting of the ways over the windows and doors between the library-dining room and catwalk. I wanted, you see, to have these double doors and windows, which reached from the floor to the ceiling, glide completely open, letting in the great outdoors. In my mind, this river-facing wall was to be very Japanesy. When the weather was nice—and I expected the weather in North Carolina to be nice all the time—there would be neither glass nor even screens between the indoors and outdoors. The doors and windows would slide behind two sets of bookcases of the same height and width as the doors and windows and disappear. At least, that's what I envisioned. But when the day came to put in the tracks for the doors and windows, the assistant couldn't understand how four doors, including the screens, could be accommodated behind each bookcase. Patiently I explained that the Japanese did it, but he wasn't impressed. I went into details, being sweet as sweet. Still he wasn't impressed. At last I wailed in exasperation, "I wish I was an architect!"

"I wish to God you were too," he shot right back. "Then you could have built this house."

One other day, when the house was all but finished, I got upset. I arrived at The Land to find the head painter putting a second coat of stain on the exterior of the house after I had specifically insisted I wanted only one. After many pros and cons, Mark and I had decided to build the house of cypress; it came from so close by—South Carolina, Georgia, and Florida—it seemed silly to go all the way to California for redwood or to the Far East for mahogany; then, too, it was more reasonable. At least that's what Ed said, though heaven knows we couldn't notice it when the bills came in. Anyway, cypress it was and Mark and I were exceedingly pleased with the look of it. Without any paint it was a fairly soft, woodsy gray with a prominent grain. I would have liked it to stay just that way, but Ed insisted it should have at least one coat of stain to preserve it. So reluctantly I agreed to that one. Then suddenly to discover a second coat being applied! Naturally, I became excited. "Take it off," I cried, sounding like that woman in the TV commercial advertising razor blades (or is it shaving cream?). "Take it all off. I want the grain of the wood to show through. Anybody can have a painted wooden house [this, of course, was a slight exaggeration, but remember I was excited]; I want the house to look as if it grew here, with knotholes and grains and . . . and whatever else it has naturally. Please, please take it off quickly before it dries."

The painter stared at me with horrified eyes.

"Please hurry," I prodded. "Every minute counts. Please get some rags right away and wipe it off."

"I have no rags," the painter said.

"No rags?" My voice rose in disbelief.

"No, ma'm. I don't carry any rags with me. I never use 'em."

"What do you use?"

"Nothing. I never have to take off any stain or paint that I put on."

"Well, I'm sorry; but this time you do need them. And if you can't get rags any other way, I'll give you my under pants."

The thought of me, an old woman, stripping right there, shocked him into protests. "That won't be necessary ma'm," he declared quickly. "I'll take off my shirt first."

"Good, you do that."

And off he took it (it was an old, faded shirt anyway) and scrubbed and scrubbed. Nevertheless, there remains a big smear, testifying to the trauma of that hour.

The staining of the outside of the house was completed before the biggest headache of the actual construction developed. That was installing in the living room the chimneyless fireplace and getting it to work without loud rumblings and great billows of smoke. The headache began when Ed learned that the factory which had made his fireplace no longer manufactured it. This, of course, should have alerted us to the alarming fact that the fireplace had been discontinued for some very good reason; but our hearts—at least mine—was set on having one. In fact, I wanted one now much more than in the beginning, for just beyond the space a chimney would occupy were two, fantastically entwined trees—an oak with a grayish-green trunk and limbs, and a slim pine. A chimney would not only block out these touchingly affectionate trees, but a broad expanse of the river.

Okay, agreed Ed; he could have the fireplace manufactured to his specifications, but it would take time. Just how much time he didn't say, for I suppose he didn't know; but for many weeks the window-door wall was held up while the carpenters waited for the fireplace to appear.

Then one morning as I walked in the front door, there it

was in the middle of the living room, looking exactly like a giant-sized coffin. It was black like only unpainted iron can be, and it was oblong, with the bottom flat and the top gently curved. It seemed the most ghastly omen. I burst into tears.

Jack and Brother George and the other workmen clustered about, trying to reassure me. They said when it was set in the glass, half inside the house and half outside on the catwalk, and when it was painted the antiqued, avocado green of the living-room woodwork, it wouldn't look so much like a coffin. Indeed, I would scarcely notice the resemblance. Just wait.

So I waited—what else could I do?—and they were right. It wasn't a thing of beauty, but it wasn't offensive either.

Now if it would only work! The "theory" calls for the smoke to be drawn by a small, concealed electric motor into the rounded hood above the fire and then down into a duct beneath the floor that carries it away. In our case, it carries it just a dozen feet or so to the chimney of the fireplace in our bedroom.

The first time we set the logs ablaze in this invention, the motor set up such a draft that, when the front door opened, it came frighteningly near drawing the person who entered straightway into the fire. We were just lucky it wasn't a small person or a grandchild. And the duct beneath the floor rattled so loudly Mark couldn't hear me speak—me, of all people, whom he claims he can hear ten miles on a clear day—and the smoke rolled out into the room and bounded to the ceiling.

Frantically we smothered the fire with dirt and telephoned dear Ed. He came, studied the situation, and made adjustments. He ordered a smaller motor and had the original duct, which was made of tin, replaced by a copper one.

Now we have a lovely fire in our wall of glass if we turn on the motor five minutes or so before we put a match to the paper and splinters so the draft will be drawing well, and if we keep the fire to the back of the fireplace and fairly small so that the volume of smoke won't be too much for the size of the duct.

This problem solved, the house itself was finished and it was even better than I had anticipated. Ed had made the "gallery" considerably wider than I had pictured it and the extra width gave the whole house a more spacious and livable air; and the catwalk, hanging out over the bluff, made the river seem closer. The only thing, we didn't make the deck big enough. When we have parties, all the guests crowd out on it until I fear the steel banisters, topped with wood, will buckle. Someday, so I say, we will add a second deck a few feet below this first one and extend it several feet farther out.

4

I didn't wait for the house to be finished to start clearing The Land. From the day we moved to Chapel Hill I began to cut diseased cherries, misshapen pines, too-crowded maples, dead elms, and other unwanted trees and blackberry briars and honeysuckle vines and other growth that flourishes on land that has never been lived on. Every morning I'd get up shortly after the crack of dawn, help the cook pack a box of sandwiches, hamburgers, and soft drinks, get in the car, and drive to a vacant lot near the center of town and pick up any man, woman, or child who was waiting there in hopes of finding a day's work. A good man was, as the old song has it, hard to find; usually I collected one or two women with children ranging from five to thirteen or fourteen years of age. They were always Negroes; white help in North Carolina is practically nonexistent.

For many weeks during that first summer I had a short, tremendously overweight, good-natured mother with a brood of five small children, who worked diligently from the time we arrived at The Land, which was usually around ten o'clock, until three-fifteen, when we sped back to Chapel Hill so they could catch a ride to their home some miles beyond with a "commuting" friend. Our late start on The Land was due to various complications. We had to stop at the icehouse and buy a block of ice for our water can—there was no water yet on The Land—and frequently we had to stop at a grocery store in Pittsboro to buy bananas or apples or grapes or watermelon and sweet crackers that the children craved. Usually all the children accompanied me into the store to assist in making the selections. Some days the mother of this flock brought along her sister or her mother, who spent all her time picking blackberries to make jelly and jam for her own consumption.

For several weeks I had a man, a strong, well-built individual with complexion the color of an old pine cone—dull black, that is—who had never had breakfast when I picked him up, so insisted on stopping at a small restaurant on the outskirts of Pittsboro to buy two hamburgers-to-go, smelling intoxicatingly of onions and meat. With him munching contentedly away on the front seat beside me, I pushed on, my mouth watering with envy. On affluent occasions he bought those little packages of orange-colored crackers spread with peanut butter, and candy bars to pass back to the "hongry" children.

Other weeks I had a very frail young man, also as black as an old pine cone, reeking with wine he'd consumed the evening before and, perhaps, even that very morning. (There were a distressing number of these winos in Chapel Hill.) At the end of each day, with the money he'd made in his pocket, he'd ask to be put off near the fanciest grocery store in this part of the world, Fowler's, to restock, as I well knew, his wine supply.

With this incongruous crew I built a stone wall, ninety-four feet long and four feet high, across the back of the house and three and a half feet away from it to hold the tons of dirt and rock the workmen excavating the basement had piled on top of patches of wild azaleas, small hollies, dogwood, and other growth.

First, we shoveled the mounds of excavated dirt and rock

against the basement foundation and then we built the wall to hold it there. We gathered in our arms (no wheelbarrow could be maneuvered on that steep grade) big rocks from all over The Land—rocks were one thing we had plenty of— and patiently and painfully fitted them without cement one on top of the other, yard by yard, day by day. I understood how the Egyptian slaves felt, building the Pyramids. Then one night a heavy rain fell and a long section of our wall collapsed. George told us we had piled our rocks too straight up and down; they should have been slanted considerably inward. We began again and went on . . . and on . . . and on. At last it was finished. Absolutely finished.

Then we laid a brick walk on the dirt we had piled inside the wall. None of us, including the wino who was working that week, had ever laid a brick walk before. In fact, in my wildest imaginings I had never dreamed of laying a brick walk. Jack and George, shaking their heads dubiously, left off building the house to show us how to level the ground and to put the bricks down in the sand. The job progressed poorly, mighty poorly, especially when the wino and I had to make two steps from one level to another. Again Jack and George appeared to give advice, but neither the wino nor I could comprehend it. Up to this writing, the steps and walk look exactly as if they were done by two winos for their own, unsteady, zigzagging feet.

The walk was a necessary adjunct to the house. As matters stood before we built it, the two doorways to the basement perched four feet above the ground with no steps leading to them. Since we had no inside basement stairs, the only way we could have got to the doors was to use stepladders. And that was the way Jack, following the architect's plans, was going to leave them.

(This was my introduction to what I consider "unfinished

business" in the construction of a house. The architect's plans cover the building of the actual house—and that's it! There are no walks to doors and steps; no leveling of hills of excavated earth; no designated parking area; no anything that's not drawn on that vital blueprint. I didn't grasp, however, the extent of the "unfinished business" when my little band and I were struggling with the rock wall. In my vast innocence I thought it was only the doors of the lowly basement that were being left up in the air.)

With the wall and walk completed, I began in earnest the clearing of the land. If I had no man, I'd saw with a small, curved-handled saw the quantities of half-grown pines and scrub oaks and gums that crowded the big trees beside the road leading to the house; but if there was a man around, I'd let him saw and the women, children and I would haul out to the road what he cut. At one point the trees and brush towered so wide and high, the carpenters and bricklayers couldn't make their way through it.

All of us preferred thinning out the jungle along the road, for the land on both sides was flat for a good ways back; it was the bluff falling to the river that gave us real trouble. Climbing up and down it was a job for goats, especially while carrying an armful of limbs or wood. Nevertheless, every tree and bush cut down had to be hauled up to the flat, open space in front of the house, where it could be burned, or hauled down to the river for the current to nose it to the Atlantic.

Inspired beyond my ordinary strength, I crawled up and slid down that 192-foot incline at least fifteen times a day. Eying my thin gray hair and sagging jowls, Jack and George and the other workmen were amazed at my climbing agility. One morning Jack approached me hesitantly, his head tucked a little to one side, and blurted out, "Mrs. Ethridge, would you mind answering a personal question?"

"Not at all," I answered heartily, trying to relieve his very evident embarrassment.

"You see, the men and I got into an argument about your age." His head ducked lower and his cheeks flamed pinker. "I asked Mrs. Abbott your age, but all she'd say was that you were old enough to collect social security. The men and I are confused and have placed bets on it."

I was tempted to answer him as my mother once answered two elderly gentlemen who had been watching her in her late eighties jump the waves at Savannah Beach. "Little lady," one of them addressed her as she came out of the water, "you have us confused. We can't decide how old you are."

"Just stay confused," said Mother and walked on briskly.

However, since I was dependent upon Jack to complete the house, I confessed to my correct age. He was pleased, for, depending on Shug's hint, he had come closest.

Some days my gang and I would turn our backs on the walls of the bluff and labor to clear a nook, lush and beautiful with hollies, dogwood, linden trees, wild azaleas, dainty, yellow-balled hypericum, and vines of every conceivable sort, on the bank of the river. I had a vision of sunbathing here with just wild flowers and the finest blooming trees encircling me. In my happy mind I even pitched a red-and-white striped tent where the children and grandchildren and friends could undress for swimming. The fact that the river at this point was humped with great stones did not disturb my dreams one whit. Someday I'd have them blown out with dynamite.

This daydreaming of mine frequently held up the job at hand. I would uncover a slope of dogtooth violets and immediately envision Confederate jasmine swinging its yellow bells above them, with paths, hemmed with primroses, circling their feet. My dreaming wouldn't have been such a road block if I had just dreamed and gone on working; but I'd drop whatever instrument I was working with and stroll about selecting the trees from which the jasmine vines would swing and stepping off the areas where the paths would wind.

Or I would come across a dry stream bed and instantly picture cool, clear water rushing along it and ferns and little wild iris crowding the banks. And again I would be off— bodily, that is—studying the lay of the land to see if a pump could be installed in Rocky and pipes laid alongside the bed as far as its beginning and there uncorked to send water gurgling back to the river.

Any flower, any tree, any rock would turn my dreams on. Once when I was dreaming out loud to a group of visitors struggling up the bluff after viewing the laurel, which was in bloom, I was jerked up short by a brash young woman. "Over here," I said airily, waving my hand to a rather bare spot, "I'm going to plant oak hydrangeas and . . ."

"If I were you," interrupted this young lady, "I'd plant benches for your guests to rest on before I did anything else."

It usually took a glimpse of the help leaning idly on the handles of their hoes and rakes or sprawled on the ground to bring me out of these enchanting trances. Then furiously I would fall to work.

Many, many hours we raked, shoveled, and pitched the thick mattress of trash in what I began to refer to as the laurel "garden." We were like old-time wheat winnowers, tossing the layers of dried reeds, sticks, hickory nuts, bottles, and heaven only knows what else back into the river from whence it had come. How many spring and fall floods had rested their heavy burdens there it is impossible to reckon; I'd settle, though, for five thousand.

Getting out the worst of this mess was backbreaking; but then there were still the weeds, vines, and trees to be rid of so the laurel could flourish. Often I'd stand, gazing upward, for ten, fifteen, or twenty minutes, trying to decide just which tree to cut down. My ignorance was monumental. I didn't know whether an oak was more precious than a maple or vice versa; or whether a sycamore was more precious than a poplar or a pine or a cedar. Some had to go, for laurel will grow in heavy shade, but it will not bloom unless it gets sun. Decisions, decisions, decisions. If only Mr. Gallup would take a poll and publish the ratings of trees.

Making paths through these thickets of laurel also took muscle and time. I shouldered my way through them like a Notre Dame quarterback, trying to spy openings that could be, with some clearing out, joined into paths. One area was so impenetrable we ended up by cutting three feet into the hillside that formed the backdrop of the laurel "preserve" to make a path.

All that summer and early fall during the building of the house I continued working with this assortment of winos, mothers, grandmothers, aunts, and children; then Mark and I moved to The Land and I had them no more.

5

We have plenty of water now, but when we were getting ready to build the house and during most of the time we were building it, we were without any and it looked for a long time as if we weren't ever going to have any. That warning not to buy land until you know you can get water, given us by our friend Morton Boyd, echoed in our ears many a day.

While we were still living on Long Island, we hired a well driller from the environs of Sanford, agreeing to pay him four dollars a foot for every foot he drilled to find a sufficient supply of water. When we next heard from him, the news was bad. Mighty bad. He declared he had gone through two hundred and fifty feet of solid rock, broken four bits, found no water, and was quitting. He couldn't afford, said he, to break any more bits.

Discouraged, we didn't hire anybody else until the house was under way. Then we contracted with another well driller, Mr. Gaines, to drill in a new spot. Before he started, however, John McKelvey, our nearest-to-be neighbor, came over one afternoon, introduced himself, and offered to locate the correct place to drill by water-witching.

"Now, Mrs. Ethridge," said he, his little blue eyes beneath bushy white brows and his peony-pink cheeks creasing into a smile, "I want you to understand I don't believe in water-witching, but it works. I was once the most skeptical of anybody in the world; but there was this time I was working for a Mr. Howard Colly in Detroit who had recently bought a farm with an awfully weak well on it. So he had a man come to drill a new well. The man—his name, I recall, was Mr. Newman—said he'd like to use a water-witch to find the best place to drill; but Mr. Colly insisted he go ahead at a spot he'd selected. Mr. Newman went down one hundred feet." Mr. McKelvey came to a dramatic stop; then shrugging, added: "No water, just clay. So Mr. Colly gave in and told Mr. Newman to proceed with the water-witch.

"Well, he got a forked apple switch—apple and peach switches are best; they carry a lot of sap. I don't know whether there's any scientific explanation, but I figure there must be some relation between the sap and the ground. Then he asked me to help him grip the stick."

Mr. McKelvey paused in his recitation for a few moments to puff a little. He had emphysema, which made him short of breath.

"You won't believe this, Mrs. Ethridge," he continued, "but we found a location in a neighbor's front yard that gave such a violent reaction it jerked the stick down toward the ground so fast it skinned the bark off right in our hands." His sharp little eyes picked at mine to see if I was properly impressed. "Well, at that point, I, who was a doubter, be-came somewhat of a believer."

"I can't blame you," I said.

"And at that spot, after drilling just forty feet, water came up within eight feet of the casing."

By this time I was chomping at the bit to get going with my own water-witch. I yearned to be a believer—a whole believer, not a "somewhat of a believer." But it took a while to quiet Mr. McKelvey down; he was, I realized, a great talker and he was on a subject in which he was well versed.

"After all, Mrs. Ethridge," he continued, "there is nothing new about a divining rod, which is all a water-witch is. In fact, it is a very old custom; just how old I can't rightly say. Moses in the Wilderness struck the rock with a divining rod, didn't he, and the water gushed out?"

"I think so," I murmured uncertainly.

"I myself was never much of a hand about the Old Testament, but I believe that was the way of it."

Having run down for the time being, Mr. McKelvey began looking about for a forked stick. There being no apple or peach available, he settled on a fairly limber hickory switch approximately three feet long. With my right hand and Mr. McKelvey's left hand clutching this above a joint and extending it horizontally straight in front of us and my left hand clasping Mr. McKelvey's right hand, we walked warily away from the shell of the house into the woods. I never felt more foolish in my life. My fervent hope, even exceeding that of discovering water, was that we wouldn't be turned into pillars of salt in that absurd, intimate coupling.

Mr. McKelvey suggested we head in the general direction of four pines that burst like mini atom bombs above the surrounding trees. He had always noticed, he explained, that where there were exceedingly tall trees there was usually a vein of water nearby.

It was rough walking. The ground was uneven—there was a deep, dry stream bed between us and the pines—and the underbrush, vines, small shrubs, and trees were almost impassably thick. Concentrating on keeping the water-witch straight out in front of us, we stumbled frequently. However, we finally approached the vicinity of the pines and then, suddenly, unmistakably, the switch reared upward, turning our hands up with it.

Happily Mr. McKelvey proclaimed: "Here, Mrs. Ethridge, you have water!"

"But I thought the switch was supposed to turn down," I protested.

"Mostly it does and the downward direction has more pull, but when it goes up, that's good too."

I wasn't one to argue with him on that.

We piled a small mound of stones at the exact spot the water-witch indicated and went rejoicing back to the house.

The next day Mr. Gaines arrived and, after being shown the divinely selected location, set up his rig and started to work. All day I could hear the air drill as it went up and down, pounding, pounding, pounding. At four dollars a foot, it sounded to my ears like the painful beating of my heart when I've run too far and too fast. Boom! Boom! Boom! All that day . . . and all the next . . . and all the next . . . and all . . . all . . . Finally Mr. Gaines announced he had gone one hundred and ninety feet, and though he had found a little water, it was not nearly enough to supply the house. I was crushed; I couldn't bear the thought of another thousand dollars down a hole; but I wasn't as crushed as Mr. McKelvey. He was still absolutely positive water was there.

With this failure, Mark was through with water-witching. In fact, he had never really got with it. He had just been patiently waiting to prove me wrong once again. He busied himself now, getting information at the University of North Carolina on where to secure professional help in this baffling business of selecting the right spot to drill a well. He learned it was very simple. All he had to do was to contact the Water Resources Board at Raleigh and they would send somebody to tell us the best place. Mark phoned, the man came, walked for a half hour or so over the land, stopped in a low-lying area near the river, and announced with perfect assurance, "This is the spot to drill."

The next day Mr. Gaines began to drill where the Water Resources man said. Pound! Pound! Pound! Dollars down! Down! Down! All over the land I could hear that air drill pounding. It sounded as if it would never, never, never stop. Yet, after days stacked on top of days, it did. At a hundred and fifty feet the water gushed up as if Moses himself had struck the rock.

6

One morning when I was working along the side of the road leading to the house, four people drove by. They glanced over at me, dripping with sweat and smeared with dirt in my blue jeans and one of Mark's discarded white shirts (poor me, I never have a new pink or blue or red or yellow or flowered blouse, just Mark's old shirts that are too raveled around the collar and cuffs for him to wear to the bank to float a loan) and floppy straw hat, and drove right on.

In a little while, however, they came back and stopped. Evidently, while they were roaming about the skeleton of the house and admiring the view, one of the carpenters had told them that that disreputable-looking old woman they had passed on the way was the owner—I mean, the half owner—of the house. Still they weren't sure.

"You are not Mrs. Ethridge, are you?" asked an elderly wisp of a gentleman, getting out of the car and coming toward me.

"I'm embarrassed to admit it, but I am," I answered and put out my hand.

"I'm happy to know you, Mrs. Ethridge. I'm Francis Le Clair." His hand in mine was slim and bony and seemingly as frail as the handle of a slat basket.

Fortunately the name rang a bell. A Chapel Hill friend, Dr. Nathan Womack, had told me that the landscape architect who had laid out the campus of the University of North

Carolina and was responsible for the magnificent specimens of shrubbery and trees around the buildings and for the glorious rose garden at the side of the Planetarium was Frances Le Clair.

I, of course, was pleased to meet him and to meet his wife, Lois, a handsome, out-doorsy, big-boned woman and the couple still sitting in the car, heads lowered, peering at me with wide, curiosity-filled eyes.

For a few minutes we chatted about the view, which they said surprised them, for though they lived only a few miles away, they never had any idea it was there. Mr. Le Clair particularly was enthusiastic about it and, as he extended his hand to say good-by, murmured, "Mrs. Ethridge, let us dream together." Not since Mark asked me to marry him had I had a happier proposal. To have someone to dream with is the greatest boon next to having someone to sleep with.

I didn't see him again for weeks. He must have waked up, I concluded, and decided not to dream with me after all. But then came the crucial time when the house, so Jack told us, was about completed. Yet there were no walks to the back kitchen door and the side porch and no definite parking area. A fairly commodious open space had been in front of the house all along; but no gravel or small rocks or pavement on it and no coping or walls of any kind to mark its boundaries. There was no planting in the patio between the two wings, though I planned to put periwinkle there; the ground was as bare as the day God created it and hilly with scooped-up clay, rocks, and even tree roots, and the side porch and open deck were suspended high in the air like a bird cage.

Frantically I called Mr. Le Clair and, reminding him of his offer to dream with me, urged him to come at once. And,

God be praised, he came and for many days thereafter, dressed immaculately in khaki shirt and pants and, in spite of the warm early fall weather, a brown tweed sports coat and tie, he hurried about the place with fast, tiny steps, studying the problems from all angles.

At noon he'd knock off work and so would I and together we'd perch like birds, he a chickadee and I a crow, on the edge of the unfinished deck, our legs and feet dangling over it, eat our hard-boiled eggs, whole tomatoes and sandwiches, and talk. Or, rather, he'd talk and I'd listen. He is a continuous talker, his almost whispered words running smoothly as a small, unimpeded brook. He usually talked about his plans to improve the house and grounds, but now and then he would reminisce about his long and colorful life.

He was born in Antwerp, Belgium, on June 21, 1884. After his public school education, he attended the Academy of Fine Arts in Antwerp and the School of Horticulture and the Tropical School of Horticulture, taking both day and night courses. During his schooling he spent one summer at Versailles, working for a landscape architect.

"It sounds big," he murmured with a twinkle in his small, gray-blue eyes, "but I was doing the dirty work; I was just the handyman."

His education completed, he came to the United States, settling for a while in Maryland. "There's where I got my first love of the United States," he declared earnestly. "That Tidewater country is very beautiful."

After Maryland, he worked for several years for nurseries in Baltimore, Philadelphia, Washington, and New York. He helped landscape and plant many of the famous estates on Long Island, among them the estate of C.K.G. Billings at Oyster Bay. This was a rush job. It had to be finished in time for a big Decoration Day "house party."

"We moved maple trees in full leaf and giant cedars and thirteen hundred rhododendrons in full bloom into the front court," he recalled with relish. "But getting the elaborate sunken garden ready on time was the most hectic and spectacular undertaking. The first three days of the very week of the party, there were between thirty and forty brick masons at work on the garden pool and terraces and walls; nevertheless, on the night of the party, when the hundred or more guests arrived, there were climbing roses blooming profusely hanging over the walls, and lilies in wide-open flower in the pool. Sounds like magic, doesn't it? But amazing things can be done when there are plenty of greenhouses and plenty of money. Of course, it takes a bit of thinking and management."

He fell silent for a brief moment, a radiant look on his narrow, deeply wrinkled face, savoring the success of that long-ago undertaking; then he added, as if reluctant to let it go: "Besides completing the gardens, we had twenty-five-foot palms in the indoor patio that was three stories high."

After World War I, he went to work for various departments of the United States government in Washington and in 1934, the Department of Agriculture sent him to North Carolina to help in the eradication of erosion and with other land-reclamation projects. Then Dr. Frank Porter Graham, the president of the University of North Carolina in those days, hired him to give all his time to the University. From his fiftieth year until his seventy-fifth, five years beyond the mandatory retirement age at the University, he devoted all his energy and time to landscaping the campus.

And now, I reflected, pleased, eleven years after his retirement he was "dreaming" with me. It was a big comedown from those estates on Long Island and the campus of

53 ह

the University; but he never once let on he considered The Land beneath his talents.

In due time he finished those undone areas around the house. With a passion for building (he really should have been an architect instead of a landscape gardener) he built walls of one sort or another everywhere possible. Under the high-up-in-the-air porch he fashioned the most enchanting curved wall, with even a seat at its base, of native stones, each one lovingly chosen for color and texture, as if they were semiprecious stones, and set them with scarcely a show of cement. In front of the two wings he erected a low brick coping to contain the Chinese holly he planned to plant there, and across the front of the patio he erected more coping to contain the periwinkle. Around the parking area, which he laid out with the greatest care, skirting the roots of dogwood and other native growth adjoining it, he built a wall of several heights, ending it on one side with steps leading to a path through the woods. When he completed this wall, the wooded area looked as if it had been elevated, for, instead of sloping down indifferently into the parking space as it had originally, it was cut off abruptly, adding seeming height, an improvement I would have never thought of.

(Since this area of woods is completely encompassed by the parking space in front of the house and another, larger parking space a little distance away, and by the roadway and the lawn, it forms a separate entity. Shug has christened it "The Social Circle" for no better reason than that is the name of a town in Georgia which has always tickled her funny bone.)

Mr. Le Clair also laid brick walks to the kitchen and porch door and made a brick-floored picnic area off the walkway in front of the porch. Also, he poured over the parking area truckloads of gray, chiplike stones, called Chapel Hill gravel, which I must say is awful on heels.

Next, he supervised the erection of a torii at the entrance to The Land. As Mark had vetoed our having a Japanese house, I was determined to have at least one of those slender, delicately curved gates that mark the approach to Shinto temples. I requested it as an anniversary present. When I told Mr. Le Clair I wanted a torii, he was transported with delight—not that he was fond of torii, but it was a challenge. He plowed through his books to find the right picture; he drew innumerable sketches; he conferred hourly with Jack, who had never heard of a torii, and with me; and he walked to and fro at the entrance, studying the pines and the lay of the land so as to select the exact right spot to place it. It had never crossed my mind that a torii required so much planning.

At last the spot was chosen, not at all where I had pictured it, close by the highway, but much more imaginatively at the top of a slight rise that the road climbs before leveling off and directly beneath a stunted pine that thrusts all its growing power to one side into two long limbs that would partly overhang the crossbeams.

When the gate was first put up, I was terribly disappointed. It was much too tall and grandiose for my taste. It looked as if it marked the entrance to a girls' or boys' camp. I felt it should have over it in huge, wooden letters, CAMP MINNEHAHA. Mr. Le Clair agreed it looked too tall but argued that if it was lower, big trucks couldn't get under it.

"I don't want any big trucks getting under it," I said.

"I wouldn't be too sure about that, Mrs. Ethridge," he advised in his soft but determined tones. "As soon as the gate is completed, you'll need cement for something and no cement mixer will be able to get under the gate."

55 ह

"I don't intend to build anything more that will call for cement."

"How about a hearse?" suggested gruesome-minded Jack. "There's a very good chance, Mrs. Ethridge, you won't live forever."

Bud, who had arrived to help unveil the gate and had been listening quietly to this argument, now spoke up. "Don't worry, if she dies"—and I thought I detected a lilt of hope in his voice—"we'll get her out if we have to tear down the gate."

Mr. Le Clair, really wanting it lower all the time, gave in, and Jack and his helpers, after sawing off the supporting posts, lowered the crossbars about half a foot. It was a big improvement.

During this rash of construction, Mark, as you can imagine, grew powerfully nervous. What was all this costing? he wondered constantly. Having never before had a landscape architect, he had not the slightest notion what Mr. Le Clair's work was worth. Five hundred dollars? One thousand? Two thousands? Three thousand? He got so he couldn't sleep at night for worrying about it.

Finally, having received no bill, he screwed up his courage and asked Mr. Le Clair right out what he owed him. "I haven't had time to figure it up yet," Mr. Le Clair murmured. "Don't concern yourself about it; I'll get around to it someday." More weeks went by without the arrival of a bill and Mark tried again; but with no better results. Then more weeks. . . .

Finally we decided to ask Dr. Womack, who we knew had had lots of experience with Mr. Le Clair, how he managed to get an accounting from him, only to learn he never had. "He won't send you a bill," Dr. Womack said. "You simply can't make him tell you what you owe him."

And the doctor was so right. Up until this hour, except

for one special commission, Mr. Le Clair has never presented us with a bill. All other times we have had to guess at what we owe him—and I'm very much afraid we are poor guessers. The one exception was for an incinerator. For months we had tried to burn papers and similar trash in those wire baskets you buy at hardware stores; but in a very few weeks they themselves burned out. After going through three or more, we decided it would be cheaper to have an incinerator built. We had had an incinerator in Kentucky: a very simple affair—a half-dozen iron rods a foot or so from the ground, enclosed by a low brick wall—about the size of a piano box.

So one morning when Mr. Le Clair appeared (after the first building spree he came infrequently and always unannounced) I mentioned we needed an incinerator and asked if he knew where I could get a half-dozen iron rods. I said I was sure we had enough brick around the place, left over from the walls and walks.

"Mrs. Ethridge, don't trouble yourself about it," he answered comfortingly. "I'll take care of it. I know were I can get some old rods and a secondhand grate [our Kentucky incinerator never heard of a grate]. Where would you like to put it?"

We walked in the woods, a hundred yards or so away from the house, and found a fairly open space below a downward curve of the land that he thought suitable.

"It's convenient to the back door," Mr. Le Clair pointed out, "yet this down slant will make it scarcely noticeable. You can forget about it now; I'll build it as soon as I can arrange for a bricklayer."

And like a fool I did forget about it until the day a big truckload of new brick showed up. "What the hell are they for?" demanded Mark, glaring as only he can glare.

"I have no idea, darling."

57 ॐ

"Don't you think to hell you've built enough around here?"

"Yes, darling, I do. You've been very generous."

"Then, goddamn it, why don't you stop? I'm already house-broke."

"I haven't even thought of building anything else, darling, except an incinerator, and you said yourself we needed an incinerator."

"God knows we don't need eight hundred bricks to build an incinerator."

"No, darling, we surely don't."

Yet, amazing as it sounds, we did.

The very next Saturday Mr. Le Clair appeared with two (2) brickmasons from the University (he is frequently able to get brickmasons and plumbers and gardeners who formerly worked for him to help him out on their days off) and they proceeded to erect what we facetiously refer to as Pharoah's Tomb. It is five feet high, twenty-one feet long, and sixteen feet wide, and is partitioned into three parts: one part completely enclosed, except at the top, is for burning trash; one part is for compost; and one part is for "standing only." After all, one does have to have a place to stand to hurl the papers and such in the incinerator and to pitchfork the grapefruit rinds, pea shells, coffee grounds, avocado peels, and other choice bits into the compost bin. The four corners of this structure are finished off with small, receding pyramids of brick, which Mr. Le Clair himself admits are "a bit much." The brickmasons without a doubt got carried away with their creation.

This once Mr. Le Clair presented Mark with the bill. It was for eight hundred dollars!

Though the cost was a shock, I contend it is worth every cent of it. Instead of being unnoticeable, as Mr. Le Clair predicted, it is the first thing guests see when they walk out on the porch or peer out of the kitchen windows. "What is that building down there in the woods?" they ask. "A guest house?" It does give The Land an air.

7

Mark and I realized very soon after his retirement that we liked retirement tremendously. How could I possibly have ever dreaded it? I don't want to sound maudlin, but retirement is simply beautiful, marvelous, idyllic. There is a great deal that is new and challenging in our North Carolina setting; yet there is no mad rush whatever, no pressure. We both feel we have served on enough boards, have headed enough drives, have begged enough money, have rung enough doorbells for political candidates, have attended enough good-cause banquets to be able to turn down any invitation that doesn't "send" us. It is as if we have been turned out into a lush, spring-green pasture to graze at will.

Our days usually follow a leisurely pattern. This doesn't mean we don't work, but we work at our own pace and at what we like. We usually wake around seven o'clock, have breakfast, and watch the *Today* program until nine o'clock. The news we get during those two hours is the only news we have until the mailman arrives around noon with the *Raleigh News and Observer*. I thought Mark would burst a blood vessel when he first realized he couldn't get a paper delivered to his door at sunrise; but, grown man that he is, he adjusted quite quickly. (Saturdays and Sundays are rough. Why CBS, NBC, and ABC television consider it permissible to shirk their business of dispensing news in the daytime during the weekends is beyond me. Newspapers and radio stations continue to provide the news; why is TV exempt?)

After the *Today* program, we turn off the big eye, dress, and go about our various interests. I either work outside, digging, weeding, planting, sawing, or I labor at the typewriter. Mark usually answers his mail (he still gets a great deal of it), writes checks, goes over his bank book, and reads. He never, never grows weary of reading. One of my more serious problems is keeping him supplied with books.

Then we take walks. Around noon every day except Sunday and holidays, he yells to me out in the woods where I'm cutting down trees or poisoning brush or doing other such work, "Willie, would you like to walk with me to the mailbox and get some exercise?" We usually walk to the mailbox—a fifth of a mile from the house—twice—first, to put our letters in the box and then, an hour later, to get other people's out. Once in a long while I can persuade Mark to hike down the glen to the laurel garden, saunter for a little way along the river, and then climb the bluff to the house.

After that, in the spring, summer, and fall and even on warm days in winter, we have our pre-lunch liquid refreshments, on our open deck, gazing at the river and at the gently undulating hills on the far side mattressed in solid green except in April and May when the green is buttoned down with rows and circles of bone-white dogwood. In winter, when the leaves are off the trees and only the pines and hollies blot the hillsides with color, we can see in the far distance two doll-like houses with bright red roofs; but at all other times there is no suggestion of habitation anywhere.

We also sit on the deck at other hours. We, especially I, could watch forever the smooth, sedate, unsuspecting span of the river approach the rocks below the bend and, reaching them, bolt upright, sputtering with frustration. My passion for staring at the river has led Bud, as soon as he reaches the house, to cry out, "Willie, look at the river!"

Early on clear evenings, which most of ours are, we see the sun, suspended almost perpendicularly above the water, glow like a round, live coal for an unpredictable space of time, then sink slowly into the trees and kindle flames of rose, cerise, orange, hot pink, green, lavender, and sundry other colors in the west, to burn until deep night. On some evenings, while the bonfire is still raging, the little new moon, as yellow and thinly sliced as a sliver of lemon, floats over the tops of the trees in the east directly behind us. On one occasion when Shug, Bud, Mark, and I were having a dinner party for young Doug Wilkinson Jr. and his bride, Elizabeth, this phenomenon in the sky brought from Bud the nicest compliment he ever paid me. "Mrs. God," he exclaimed, "you have wrought another miracle."

The remark sounded a bit shocking, but I knew Bud couldn't be intentionally sacrilegious. He is always, so it seems to me, what I in my absent-minded fashion speak of as the "first warden"—he is really the senior warden, of his church. But even if it is sacrilegious to say so, I must confess that I often feel like Mrs. God, sitting on the deck with the beautiful North Carolina woods spread out below me. And I suspect Mark believes he is Mr. God and that every day is the seventh.

But to go back to the before-lunch drinking hour so that I can get to lunch and move on, we have that so-called midday meal at 1:30 and as we have it we watch (now don't laugh) *As the World Turns* and at 2 *The Newlywed Game.* Mark at first resisted *As the World Turns,* but finally I broke him down. I had got hooked two years before while living in Garden City and having my lunch alone. When the *Newlyweds* fade out, we turn off the TV and I go back to my gardening or writing and Mark takes a nap. If anything prevents or interrupts his nap, Mark is cross; terribly cross.

One winter afternoon when I came in from my labors, his steely blue eyes lanced through me and he snapped, "Remember, when you started out, you said, 'Take a long nap, darling'?"

"Yes, I remember," I answered.

"Well, I came in here [I'd made it into the bedroom before the outburst] and decided not to read the paper as I usually do, but to go straight to bed. And when I had just that minute lain down, Joe [he was a substitute yard man] knocked on the front door and said, 'Mr. Ethridge, Mrs. Ethridge said for you to tell me where the faucets are so I can get some water for the flowers.' So I went out and tried both faucets in front of the house, but no water came out. So I told him, 'There are no damn faucets working. And what's more, Mrs. Ethridge knows there are no damn faucets working.'"

He glared at me with heightened ferocity, but I felt it was more pretense than real. "Why in hell did you send him up to ask me where the faucets are?"

"I didn't, darling," I protested. I knew we had turned off the pump on the river when the cold weather came so it wouldn't freeze.

"I then took a six-minute nap—six minutes by the clock," he continued, "and then Joe was back, knocking on the door very politely and saying, 'Mr. Ethridge, Mabel [Shug's maid whose mother often does ironing for us] sent these sheets.' Half asleep as I was, I thought he said, 'these cheeses' and took the bag and carried it all the way to the kitchen before I found out they were sheets. Then I went back to sleep.

63 ॐ

Seven minutes later—seven minutes by the clock—Joe appeared again and said, 'I've got to have five dollars to get the saw sharpened and I want to borrow five dollars until payday. Mrs. Ethridge said to tell you to let me have it.'

"Then, when I had slept four more minutes—four minutes by the clock—Shug called me and said, 'How are you, Father?'

"I said, 'I'm fine.'

" 'What you doing?' she said.

" 'I was sleeping, damn it.'

"Then she said, 'Where's Mother?'

" 'Out in the woods, of course,' I said.

" 'Daddy, you know those flares the Wyatts gave you and Mother for Christmas?'

" 'Faintly,' I said.

" 'Well, will you have Joe get them out from wherever they are and fill them with kerosene and bring them in for our party Saturday night?'

" 'Where in hell am I going to get kerosene?' I asked.

" 'Oh, just anywhere, Daddy.'

"By this time it was time for *Perry Mason*." He glared at me again and mimicked, " 'Take a long nap, darling.' Hell, I got seventeen minutes by the clock. Ss-ss-ss-ss [he sounded like an enraged gander hissing; it is a habit he has taken up recently]. God a-mighty! And the doctor told me to get an hour and half nap a day."

After his nap—that is, if he gets one—he raids the refrigerator and the kitchen shelves for something to eat, ending up usually with peanut butter and saltine crackers. Though I'm tempted to murmur, "the poor dear," I can't, for he adores peanut butter and saltines. Next to sardines, they are his favorite food. He has those delicacies with a glass of milk and, unless we are invited out to dinner, he eats nothing more until breakfast the next morning.

When I knock off work around 5:30, I, too, find something simple to stave off starvation, but not peanut butter and saltines, and with my repast on a tray settle down with Mark to listen to the local newscaster at six o'clock, and then, at 6:30, to the best broadcaster of them all, Walter Cronkite. After Walter, we watch those programs that interest us or turn the TV off and read. After an eight-hour day in the woods or at my desk, I'm frequently dead to the world by 8:30; but Mark, benefiting from his afternoon nap, manages to stay awake until after the eleven o'clock news.

Mark sometimes gets so carried away with what he has seen and, incidentally, shared with me on television that he speaks with exclamation marks in his voice. One Saturday, in the middle of the day, we saw a most thrilling, close-fought basketball game between North Carolina State and the University of Maryland; then later in the afternoon, a formidable football battle between the Washington Redskins and the Miami Dolphins that so excited Mark he demanded of me again and again, "Don't I show you everything? Don't I take you everywhere?" Having been no farther than the mailbox for a week, I couldn't truthfully say, "Yes, darling, you do"; but he wouldn't have heard me if I had.

You have gathered, I'm sure, from the above recital that the TV has become very important to us in our retired lives. In fact, I can't imagine what retired people of past eras did in the evenings to entertain themselves. When our set blows a tube or for some other mysterious reason goes on the blink, we are lost. Quickly Mark phones Bud, who he feels should know all about TV sets because of his radio station, and urges him to send help RIGHT NOW. For two years Bud dispatched his own engineer, a lovable, drawling, slow-moving human, Pat Patterson, but just before Christmas one year Bud transferred Mark's call to a store that specializes in television sets and other appliances.

The repairman said he would have to take our set into Sanford to correct the trouble; however, he would leave us a new Zenith he had thoughtfully brought out for us to use in the meantime. Mark, naturally, didn't know how to work the new Zenith—in truth, Mark doesn't know how to work anything—if his bedside light blows, he moves to another room—so every time the picture of the set wasn't as clear as he thought it should be or the faces of the actors were tinged with purple he would call Bud and splutter with considerable fury, "You tell those television people to come out here and get this goddamn cheap set and bring our own set back."

"All right, Pop," Bud would say soothingly. "I'll tell 'em."

When a few days would pass without the old set being returned, Mark would telephone Bud again. "Where the hell is our television set? I'm goddamn tired of this cheap, good-for-nothing substitute those people left out here."

"Pop, you must remember it is right before Christmas," Bud would explain. "This is their busiest season."

And so it went until after all the presents had been distributed from under the tree Christmas morning, with Mark and me receiving practically nothing. Then, only then, Bud said, "Pop, Willie, to get your present you'll have to follow me."

Oh, dear Lord, I thought with dismay, the children have given us an outdoor grill and there is nothing, but nothing, Mark will loathe more. He believes outdoor cooking is for barbarians and nomads.

But to my relief Bud, with all the children and grandchildren at his heels, didn't head for the outside but turned to the right toward our bedroom. The happy thought then flashed into my mind that they had had Mark's portrait painted. However, when my eyes scanned the walls there was no portrait, not even a new picture; just the same thirty or more old ones of the members of the family.

Excitedly I searched the room. Maybe a new pair of bedspreads we needed desperately. Or maybe a new rug, which we also needed desperately. But no, the same old darned white chenille spreads lay crumpled at the foot of the beds and the same old worn, spotted, and faded blue rug lay on the floor. What could it be? I saw nothing different about the room, nor, evidently, did Mark who was staring everywhere too. Then I noticed among the clutter of photographs on top of the TV set a big gold bow and, suspended from it, a strip of white paper with names written on it. The children had given us that "damn cheap set." We were flabbergasted. It was a much, much bigger gift than they could afford.

And how perfectly they had kept the secret! No one had given us a hint, not even dear, hard-pressed Bud. In his amazement Mark turned to that once-upon-a-time hellion, Mary Schneider, now at this Christmastime eight years old and muchly improved, and asked, "Mary, did you know about this?"

"Yes, sir."

"How long have you known about it?"

"Ever since Mama and Daddy cut off my allowance."

Now we watch television with even more enjoyment than before, but not, according to Mark, with any clearer picture. He doesn't give up easily.

*

8

The fact that I'm enjoying Mark's retirement much more than I expected doesn't mean he's changed enough to notice. I don't suppose I'd like it if he had changed. After all these many years together, I'm sure I'd be frightened if he weren't basically his same old self. That beautiful dream I had of him working side by side with me in the garden and woods has faded completely. Mark never has liked physical labor or any kind of outdoor work and he still doesn't. If he hadn't had a good mind and known how to use it, the children and I would have starved to death long ago.

But I didn't give up my dream without a struggle. Indeed, after we first settled in, I urged him constantly to come out and help. Finally, though, after an exchange that made me realize I was fighting a lost cause, I stopped. "Please, darling, come with me to the woods and help me just a little while," I coaxed. "You'd enjoy it if you tried it."

"No," he answered emphatically. "I didn't retire to become a day laborer."

"What's wrong with being a day laborer?" I retorted. "That's the most snobbish remark I ever heard you make. I'm a day laborer and I'm proud of it."

"Well, you go right on being a day laborer. Nobody's stopping you."

And he meant just what he said, especially the remark that nobody was stopping me. He doesn't mind my working from nine o'clock in the morning until dusk. In fact, he not only doesn't object—he brags about it. One afternoon when we were buying tomatoes and corn from a neighbor who grows his own, the neighbor asked, "Don't you have a garden, Mr. Ethridge?"

"No," Mark replied, "but my wife has a big one. Mostly flowers, though." Then, gesturing toward me, he boasted, "I have a real work horse there."

"Yes," assented the vegetable man pleasantly, "I can see you have."

Mark even gives me presents to encourage me in my labors. Our first Christmas on The Land he gave me a power saw to make cutting down trees easier; but he also added a pair of seventeen-inch-long white kid gloves and a bottle of Joy. I accepted this incongruous assortment as a compliment; evidently I'm everything to him.

One red-letter day, though, for a very little while, he came close to stepping out of character. I was deep in the holly grove, sawing away at a crooked pine sapling when Mark appeared and stood nearby, eying me in a rather absent-minded fashion. I was kneeling on the ground, back bent far over, pushing and pulling at the hand saw, pushing and pulling, pushing and pulling. It was a tough tree, moist with sap and turpentine, and the saw kept sticking. After about ten minutes Mark sauntered over, rested the palm of his right hand on the bole of the tree, and leaned gracefully forward. This ballet pose wasn't sufficient to bend the pine a fraction of an inch; nevertheless, surprisingly, it did stop the saw from sticking and in no time the blade cut through and the pine toppled.

"I helped a lot, didn't I?" asked Mark.

"Oh, yes, darling, you were wonderful."

Immediately I hurried to another pine that was smothering a young holly, bent knees to the ground, and put the saw to the rough brown bark. Again Mark sauntered over and assumed his leaning pose. I was so pleased I could scarcely saw; this was the cooperation of which I had dreamed!

Three times he did it. Three! Then, sighing exaggeratedly and putting on an act as if he were sagging into a bed of pine needles, he announced: "That's it. I have to go in the house now and rest. I'm pooped." He should have said, of course, "bored."

That ended his Tower-of-Pisa act, not only for that morning, but for all time. In truth, he seemed to backslide. Shortly afterward we had a terrific thunderstorm and when it was past, I asked Mark to take a walk with me to see what damage had been done. "Okay, I'll give you a half hour," he agreed. "But I want it understood—no picking up limbs."

Still, I must give him his due. He has cooperated in less strenuous roles. I invited him one afternoon to go with me to the Farmers' Cooperative to buy some hose.

"Does the Farmers' Cooperative sell hose?" he asked.

"Certainly. The Farmers' Cooperative sells practically everything—electric frying pans, irons, boots, rope, hams, barbed wire . . . you name it, they sell it."

"All right. Let's go now and get it over with."

At the Cooperative he decided to stay in the car and listen to the radio while I shopped. Finding the light-weight, plastic hose I wanted, I bought 1,065 feet, which was the amount I had to have if it was to reach from the faucet by the house to the roses along the banks of the highway at the entrance to The Land. As I had no charge account at the time at the Cooperative, I returned to the car and told Mark I had to have $89.75.

"Did you say eighty-nine seventy-five?" he all but shouted.

"Yes, eighty-nine seventy-five."

"My God," he wailed, "how many pairs did you buy?"

Another time I needed a sprayer. I had discovered that the wild azaleas Mr. Le Clair had set out along the path leading through the glen to the laurel garden were being eaten up by some horrid varmint. The leaves were so chewed over they resembled pale-green lace. And, naturally, at that critical moment, the old sprayer sprang a leak.

"Please, Mark darling, hurry to the Farmers' Cooperative and get me a new sprayer," I urged. "I'd go myself, but I can't spare the time. I've got to spray every second with the old sprayer until you get back."

He returned with pleasant promptness, but he had a sort of hang-dog air. I realized something had happened that embarrassed him. After considerable questioning he confided that when he asked the salesman for a sprayer, the salesman had brought him a big can that had to be strapped on the back. "Isn't that too heavy?" Mark questioned.

In surprise, the salesman eyed Mark's ruddy cheeks and fairly stalwart, compact figure; then, in a voice that soared upward with incredulity asked, "For *you*, sir?"

"No," answered abashed Mark. "For my wife."

But in spite of refusing to help on The Land, he is slowly learning about the problems that beset it. One evening he told me a joke from the *Reader's Digest* that was quite revealing. "This man was mowing his lawn," Mark related, "and he heard the crab grass singing *We Shall Overcome*."

See? He actually knows about crab grass!

Though he hasn't turned over enough new leaves to make me feel I'm living with a stranger, he has changed in two small, wondrous ways. He now and then helps me around the house and he shops for groceries. As he was a lowly gob the first few months in the navy during the First World War, he doesn't consider beneath him any task he performed then, such as swabbing our catwalk and deck and mopping the loggia around the patio. And every weekend, when we have no domestic help, he actually washes the breakfast dishes so I can get to my outside jobs. One Monday morning, after two days of washing dishes, he announced plaintively that he had "dishpan hands." He also empties the trash.

His shopping for groceries, however, is the greatest transformation. He has always despised shopping of any kind. All our married lives I've never been able to get him into a store. If we happened to be downtown on our way to a movie and I had to step into a shop to buy something, he remained outside, even if it was raining, sleeting, and snowing. Once in San Francisco he spent the morning on the sidewalk in front of that fabulous store, Gumps, while I browsed inside. Only once has he even shopped for a Christmas present for me; he has always made Shug do his Santa Claus buying. The result of his one attempt I must admit was enough to discourage him. He bought me a gauzy, black chiffon gown with a deep yoke of lace that I couldn't possibly wear and feel decent in. I simply had to return it—the only time I ever returned one of his gifts.

"I just can't wear this gown," I explained to the clerk behind the lingerie counter in Bycks in Louisville.

She removed it from its tissue and spread it out. Then, slowly shaking her head, she said, "Mrs. Ethridge, I can't imagine who Mr. Ethridge was thinking of when he bought this."

Well, that ended Mark's shopping career until now, when he sallies forth blithely three or four times a week to shop either in the A & P or Winn-Dixie in Sanford or at Piggly Wiggly or Pete's Market in Pittsboro. He pushes around one of those wire carts, filling it with items on the list I have made out and items I never thought of putting on the list. On his return he calls gaily, "Willie, I brought you a surprise!" And a surprise it is. If I'm dieting, which I have to do frequently, he brings avocados, ice cream, cans of sardines packed in oil, spareribs, pork chops, cans of creamed soups (he's mad about creamed soups), and baskets and baskets of okra, of which he is also madly fond.

Furthermore, he brings the exciting news of Pittsboro and Sanford. He sees many of our women friends shopping too, and he stops and chats with them cozily. After one buying spree he announced, "Willie, this is a big day in Pittsboro."

"Really?"

"Yes, the new Fords came out. The minute I went into Pete's a woman whose name I don't know but whose face is familiar asked, 'Mr. Ethridge, have you seen the new Fords yet?'"

9

Though Mark is of little assistance to me outdoors or in the house, I do have a wonderful helper, a young Negro woman, Lucille Graham. She has a beautiful face as round as the full moon, with enormous black eyes and white teeth; but she's terribly overweight. She weighs at least two hundred and fifty pounds.

We worry constantly about her weight; we are scared to death she will have a heart attack. One afternoon when I was writing in the library-dining room I heard the most blood-curdling groans coming from the service area of the house. With shaking knees I rushed to the kitchen—I was sure the feared attack had hit. But when I reached the kitchen, Lucille wasn't there. The groans were coming from the bedroom back of the kitchen that, since we have no sleep-in maid, we use for ironing, a playroom for the grand-children when they come, a dressing room for Lucille, and for a variety of other activities.

I hurried toward it and, reaching the door, I saw an al-most nude Lucille standing upright, her two feet planted at least a yard and a half apart, her fists clutching the top of a girdle as she struggled mightily to pull it over her bulging thighs, and her mouth wide open emitting those ghastly groans. Basically she was a tragic figure; nevertheless, in my relief I burst into laughter. And so did Lucille. Her stretched legs pinioned in the girdle, she doubled over, all but collapsing to the floor, and let out breathless whoops of merriment.

I wasn't surprised that she saw the humor in the situation. She has a high risibility threshold and she's not sensitive in the least about her size or her appetite. One day, after midday dinner, when Bud went into the kitchen and found her consuming a soup bowl full of blueberry cobbler, he said, "Lucille, you don't need that cobbler."

"Why, Mr. Abbott, I don't eats much," Lucille protested. "I eats just like a bird."

"That's right, Lucille. Peck after peck after peck."

Her shouts of laughter could be heard in Pittsboro.

In this race-conscious age, when all sensitive whites anxiously watch their tongues for fear they may let slip a remark unintentionally hurtful to blacks, Bud says the most audacious, really shocking things to Lucille and gets the most appreciative response. Evidently she understands he couldn't care less about the color of her skin. She knows, too, I'm sure that a Puerto Rican couple, black as the back of a chimney, who recently moved to Sanford and joined the all-white Episcopal Church, St. Thomas, to which Bud and Shug belong, asked Bud, much to his delight, to be the godfather of their son and that, after the christening service, he and Shug had a champagne party in honor of the occasion at their house. Also, Lucille knows that Bud has served on several citizen committees to ease the tension caused by the integration of the schools in his county and that he is regarded by the blacks in Sanford as their best white friend.

One recipe Lucille has never been able to master is white sauce. She makes a runny mess of it every time she tries. "That's perfectly okay, Lucille," Bud assures her. "Why should you know how to make white sauce? What you know how to make is black sauce. And that's the way it should be."

Guffaws rise from the depths of Lucille's ample stomach.

Lucille cooks two meals a day, five days a week. She arrives on the dot of seven o'clock. In winter it is still night and I'd prefer her to come later, but she likes to get off by three and so persists in traveling the ten miles from Sanford, where she lives, to The Land in eerie darkness. Her one shortcoming, as far as I'm concerned, is that she will not work on Sundays during her church hours. Even if President Nixon were to come to our house on Sunday (God forbid) she'd still refuse to darken our door until after her morning church service.

She's a Jehovah's Witness and worships in what she calls "Kingdom Hall"—not a church. There are thousands of Jehovah's Witnesses in North Carolina, according to Lucille; indeed, there are millions all over the world.

"We have Jehovah's Witnesses in every yuke and jam in every part of the world," she bragged to me one day.

"Yuke?" I questioned. "How do you spell 'yuke'—y-u-k-e?"

"I suppose so," she answered, smiling a great big smile that almost split in equal halves her whoop-round face.

"And just what do Jehovah's Witnesses believe?"

"Our religion is completely based on the Bible. My family and I were Presbyterians before we became Jehovah's Witnesses, but the Presbyterians didn't live up to Bible standards. We try not to sway in any way from the Bible teachings or arrangements. We don't take any part in political campaigns or voting; we stand neutral where such worldly things are concerned. We are followers of Jesus Christ and we are going to do the same way He did. He didn't participate in politics and such stuff as that. He didn't do it because He was supposed to be our president; he was elected by God as our head; but way back in ancient times, the Pharisees and Sadducees . . ."

"The Sadducees?" I inquired, never having heard of them.

"Yes, the Sadducees and the Pharisees rebelled against a God they couldn't see. They said they had no God but Caesar, which meant man, and because of the hardness of their hearts God let them have their own way and Jesus returned to heaven and took His side by Jehovah God, His Father."

This last remark reminded me that Lucille had become outraged with me the first Christmas she was with us when I asked her to help me hang two wax figures of the Virgin holding the Christ child, mounted on heavy gold paper.

"The idea of you, Mrs. Ethridge, showing Jesus as a little baby," she had snorted. "He was thirty-three and a half years old when he died and that was two thousand years ago."

"Lucille, you mean Jesus is now two thousand and thirty-three and a half years old?"

"No, but he ain't no baby," she retorted. "When He died, He became a spirit; He didn't age any more. He's immortal—that means you don't age. He died for all time."

"Was Jesus black?" I asked. "Or was he white or yellow or some other color?"

"He was an Ethiopian and so he was brown," she answered with certainty.

Lucille not only frowns upon depicting Jesus as a baby in the Virgin's arms, she disapproves of Christmas itself. "I don't believe in Christmas," she announced that first year, "because it has a pagan origin."

Half teasingly I said, "That's great, Lucille; we won't have to give you any presents."

Her immense eyes rolled upward and she laughed good-naturedly. "You're wrong there. I likes to receive gifts of appreciation."

The only holiday Lucille observes as far as her religion goes is the day marking Jesus' death. "We don't celebrate any pagan holidays, not even birthdays. The only day any Christian is supposed to celebrate is Jesus' death. 'Do this each year in remembrance of me,' Jesus said. 'Just do it once a year.' This is the only day the Bible tells us to celebrate."

Nevertheless, Lucille believes in taking off New Year's Day, Labor Day, Veterans Day, and Thanksgiving. Those days have nothing to do with her religion; they pertain only to her job, which is an entirely different matter.

I agree, of course, for her to be off. She may not be with us much longer in the role of cook and maid and so I feel I must do all I can to make life pleasant for her while we have her. You see, this "wicked system" under which we are now living is coming to an end in 1975. Lucille's Bible tells her so and she has passed the word on to me.

"According to the chronological count of time," she said glibly, "the Bible shows that 1975 will be the end of mankind's six thousand years of existence. We Jehovah's Witnesses are not saying that's the end of the world, but just the same, the Bible doesn't go beyond 1975."

"You really believe that, Lucille?"

"It's not what I believe; it's what the Bible says and who am I to contradict the Bible?" She threw out her hands, palms upward, and shrugged her heavy shoulders slightly. "The Bible says when this wicked system ends God is going to ersher in this new Paradise like we had before Adam and Eve sinned in the Garden of Eden."

"What will it be like?"

"It will be like Paradise, and Paradise means perfection. Everybody will be living on earth like one big happy family. And we'll be living forever and ever, without end. Everything in the new order will be perfect. No sickness, no pain, no sorrow. Revelation, chapter twenty-one, verses three and four, tells us how God is going to do away with everything that causes sorrow or pain. . . . Wait a minute . . . I'll read it to you."

She waddled down the hall to our bedroom and found, I'm glad to say, a Bible and returned bearing it like a platter of food in her two outstretched hands. Expertly she turned the tissue-thin pages until she came to the passage she had cited. In melodious, Kingdom Hall tones, she read:

" 'And I heard a great voice out of heaven saying, Behold, the tabernacle of God is with men, and he will dwell with them, and they shall be his people, and God himself shall be with them, and be their God.

" 'And God shall wipe away all tears from their eyes; and there shall be no more death, neither sorrow, nor crying, neither shall there be any more pain: for the former things are passed away.' "

"That certainly sounds wonderful."

"Yes, it's great to look forward to."

"I suppose when that time comes you won't be working for us any more?" I suggested.

She gave a little whinny-like laugh. "I don't know about that, but I do know God didn't make man to be lazy. Ezekiel says it's going to take seven years just to clean up the world—clean up all the bodies and bones of the wicked ones Jehovah God will destroy when He comes."

Lucille is so sure all this is coming to pass that one afternoon when I asked a very smart young black who was washing our walls whether he was going to college when he finished the Sanford High School he was attending, Lucille scowled darkly and muttered, "He's one of us and we don't want him to go to college."

Seeing it was a touchy subject, I didn't pursue the matter

then, but a few days later I reintroduced it. "Why did you say the Jehovah's Witnesses didn't want Milton to go to college?"

"Because if he went to college now he wouldn't have time to finish," she answered promptly. "But even if he did finish and became a lawyer or a teacher or a doctor or a mortician, we wouldn't have any need for him in the Paradise on earth. It's better for him to spend the next few years serving God and making sure he's one of the chosen to continue living on this earth forever."

Being "chosen to continue living on this earth forever," however, is not the top priority among the Jehovah's Witnesses. The real élite have already gone to the "heavens" or are going someday soon.

"In the fourteenth chapter of Revelation, seventh verse, it explains that there are a hundred and forty-four thousand who are going to the 'heavens,'" Lucille told me calmly, "while the rest stay on this earth."

Bewildered, I said, "Lucille, I don't know what you're talking about. Who chooses these hundred and forty-four thousand?"

"God chose them hundreds of years ago, even before the Flood." She sounded amazingly matter-of-fact. "As long as the Bible has been written, they were chosen. God knew from the very beginning who they were and they are now all in heaven, except a few. At the last count I believe there were just four thousand left on earth."

I was more dumbfounded than ever. "Who counts them?" I quavered. "Who knows who are among the chosen?"

"Each congregation counts those who partake of the unleavened bread and wine at the Lord's Supper."

"Don't you partake of the Lord's Supper? Don't all the members of the congregation?"

"No, just those who are among the four thousand."

"But how do they know they belong to the four thousand?"

"That's between them and Jevovah God. There's something inside them that lets them know they're numbered among the four thousand. It's the spirit of God that tells 'em."

"How do they differ from all the other Jehovah's Witnesses?"

"They are virgin in every respect. They haven't fouled themselves with loose conduct or immoral acts. They lead pure, clean lives just as Jesus did."

I shook my head, but Lucille was not disturbed by my bewilderment. "Do these chosen ones die before they go to heaven?" I asked.

"Yes, they have to die, because the Bible tells us no blood and flesh can enter heaven. That's why Jesus had to die before He ascended back into heaven."

"Are any of these four thousand, who are still on earth, members of your congregation in Sanford?"

"No."

"I don't see why you, Lucille, aren't one of the four thousand; you are so good and go to church every time the door is opened."

"I don't want to be one of the four thousand," she answered surprisingly. "I'd rather go on living here on earth forever and ever and ever."

"You mean you're never going to die?"

"I don't know what's going to happen to me before 1975, but if I do die before Jehovah God comes, He'll resurrect me. Everyone who remains faithful to the end will be resurrected. The Thirty-seventh Psalm, verses ten and eleven, tells how God is going to destroy the wicked ones, but the

81 ⧼

righteous ones will be left. Then verse twenty-nine tells how the earth will be desolated, but it will always be inhabited—that's God's purpose. Now to explain that . . . Matthew six, beginning, I believe, with verse eight or nine —I'm not sure which . . . shows how we are to pray for God's kingdom to come and His will be done here on earth as it is in heaven, so if He's going to destroy the earth, why would He have his people pray for it to be preserved?"

"I don't know," I admitted.

Lucille laughed softly but, nevertheless, gloatingly.

"Those who die in His favor will be resurrected back to everlasting life right on this earth," she repeated.

"Are whites Jehovah's Witnesses too?"

"Certainly. Why, there might be more whites than blacks. I'm not sure about the number, but there are plenty of whites."

"In your Sanford congregation?"

"Yes, a lot of 'em. Everybody meets together. We eats together and we sleeps together. We don't have any social distinctions. Nobody is above anybody else."

I saw for myself this last assertion was true when, a few weeks after this conversation with Lucille, her mother died and Mark, Shug, Bud, and I went to the funeral at Kingdom Hall on the outskirts of Sanford. Except for all the benches in the middle of the hall, which were filled to overflowing with Lucille's huge family (she is one of ten brothers and sisters), there were many whites sprinkled among the congregation and the service was conducted by a young, impressive, white minister, Terry Smola, who has lived in Sanford for fifteen years.

I also saw other evidence to prove that Lucille and the members of her family really believe the tenets of the religion they practice. They were so confident they would be reunited with their loved one—and that time not far off—there was no weeping, no outward sign of grief whatever. In fact, Lucille's face, whenever I glimpsed it, was wreathed in smiles. Adding to the air of . . . well, not quite happiness, but certainly bordering on it . . . the flowers were brought in in a procession preceding the coffin by a dozen or more female "flower bearers" who were, as the printed program explained, "friends of the family."

The service was simple and unbelievably civilized. There was no music and in the "funeral discourse" there was neither eulogy nor condolence, only expressions of hope. With a minimal number of words of his own, the minister read in a quiet, unemotional manner verses from various Books of the Old and New Testament pertaining to man's creation, life, death, and resurrection. So quickly and easily did he leaf through the pages that I was amazed at how at-home he was with the Scriptures.

At the cemetery, the service, which was conducted by a black, was simple too, and when it was over, the Negroes mingled among the whites, including Mark, Shug, Bud, and me, with complete naturalness, introducing themselves, shaking hands, and explaining their connections with "Sister" Graham.

On the way home the four of us were full of admiration at the manner in which the Jehovah's Witnesses conducted their funerals; but still I wasn't moved to accept their beliefs, especially the belief that the "wicked system" we have now is coming to an end in 1975. Selfish as I am, I don't want to believe it. I'm afraid our chances of keeping dear Lucille in the kitchen will be pitifully slim. And the kitchen is not my idea of Paradise.

10

One Saturday morning, after we had lived on The Land for six months, I left off cutting down trees and grubbing up blackberry roots to go with Mark to register. He had read in the *Raleigh News and Observer* that the polling places would be open that Saturday for newcomers to the state and new voters to register. We started out bright and early for Pittsboro, the seat of our county of Chatham, resolved to be loyal, upright Tar Heels.

(Incidentally, I had just learned why North Carolinians are called Tar Heels. The reason is so obvious I don't know why I hadn't figured it out for myself; however, I hadn't, and it came as a pleasant surprise when I read it in the tome, *North Carolina, The History of a Southern State,* by Hugh Talmadge Lefler and Albert Ray Newsome. These authors say that when the state was still a young colony it developed two industries, naval stores and lumber, as well as several lesser industries based on forest products.

("The most significant commercial industry was naval stores—tar, pitch, rosin and turpentine," they write. "In fact, North Carolina led the world in the production of naval stores from about 1720 to 1870, and it was this industry that gave to North Carolina its nickname, 'Tar Heel State.' In the eighteenth century, seven-tenths of the pitch exported from all the colonies to England came from the long-leaf pine forests of North Carolina.")

North Carolinians are extraordinarily politically minded. As I had already discovered, dozens and dozens of candidates seek office at every election. At times it seems there will be nobody left to vote. The papers are crammed with who is running for what and, to a lesser degree, who has decided not to run for what. Our friends and acquaintances talk politics more animatedly than they do illnesses and scandals.

Yet, registering to vote is handled in the most casual fashion. Arriving at the Chatham County courthouse, Mark and I wandered about until we found a room occupied by a stout middle-aged woman and a skinny elderly man whom we judged from the sign on the door to be registrars; and so they were. But they were not our registrars—only the people who live in the precinct in which Pittsboro is located are eligible to register there, the woman told us; we must register in our own precinct.

"But what is our precinct?" Mark asked.

"Where do you live?" the woman questioned.

Mark told her. She, looking blank, shook her head and the old man shook his head too. "I don't know what precinct you are in," she said, "but I'll try to find out for you." She excused herself and went out. In a few minutes Mark followed her, leaving me with the old man. He talked to me cozily about his second wife, though how we got on this intimate subject I'll never know. She was a splendid woman, that I do know. An exceptionally fine woman who took the very best care of him. He had nothing to complain about. Then he moved on, or rather back, to his first wife. She gave him nothing to complain about either. Then on to his children and grandchildren and the farm on which he lived and innumerable other subjects.

After twenty or so minutes Mark and the woman returned. We lived, Mark informed me, in the Oakland-Asbury Church precinct. The Asbury Church part didn't come as a surprise. I had been thinking while listening to the old man that we might be in the Asbury Church precinct, for often, as we approached The Land from Pittsboro, I'd noticed with considerable interest a sign, "Entering The Asbury Church Community," and I had seen on a country road leading off our highway the Asbury Church itself, an inposing red brick building with a large graveyard and huge oak trees.

The church was named, as I knew, for Francis Asbury, the first bishop of the Methodist Episcopal Church to be consecrated in America. My interest in him was stirred because he had been a friend of John Wesley, the subject of the book *Strange Fires* that I was working on at the time.

I had even looked up Mr. Asbury in the *Encyclopedia Britannica* and in Messrs. Lefler's and Newsome's *North Carolina* and learned that there was no official Methodist Church in the United States until after the Revolution. And it looked for a while that there would never be a Methodist Church, for John Wesley at the beginning of the Revolution had almost "done it in." In what he termed his "Calm Address," he had pleaded with his friends and followers to remain loyal to England and, alas, many of them followed his advice. This "stigmatized" the Methodists in America and made them woefully unpopular. What few churches had been formed were closed and the "activities of the Methodist societies were greatly restricted." But then, in 1780, Francis Asbury made a "missionary tour" through the United States, which included North Carolina, restoring respectability to the Methodists and putting new life into their labors. It was during this tour, on July 22, that he visited our Rocky River area and organized the church that bears his name.

"But where do we register?" I asked the woman.

She shook her head. She knew the name of our registrar, a Mr. Burns, but neither she nor her co-worker had the slightest notion where Mr. Burns set up shop for performing this service. For several silent moments they mulled the matter over; then the woman remembered there was a country store run by a Mrs. Johnson near the Asbury Church.

"Oh, we know Mrs. Johnson well," I caroled. "We often shop at her store when we run out of eggs, butter, milk, and other necessities." (Unfortunately for us, it closed soon afterward.)

"That's good," said the woman. "You go there and Mrs. Johnson might be able to tell you where Mr. Burns is registering new voters, or if she can't tell you, maybe somebody sitting around the store can."

Armed with this dearly bought information, Mark and I retraced our steps to Rocky River, then continued on for a few miles to Mrs. Johnson's. Yes, Mrs. Johnson knew Mr. Burns and she knew he was registering people this very day; but just where he was registering, she wasn't sure. Most likely at his house, though, for that was where he usually registered voters.

She proceeded to give us detailed directions on how to get to Mr. Burns's house. We were to go to the end of the road on which the store was located; turn to the right; pass the Asbury Church; then at the first dirt road turn left and continue until we came to a brick house on the left. It was easy to find, she assured us, and no great distance.

We took the dirt road to the left and rode . . . and rode . . . and rode. We passed several houses shortly after turning on the dirt road, but then we saw none at all. "It couldn't be this far," Mark and I kept saying to each other. "Why, we've come miles and miles."

Finally we glimpsed a house on the left, a quarter of a mile back from the road, but it wasn't brick. It was wood, painted white, with big trees around it. "That couldn't be it," I argued. "Mrs. Johnson said it was brick and anyway, it's too far from the store. She said it was no distance. We must have taken the wrong turn. Maybe we should have turned to the left when we came to that dead end before we got to the Asbury Church."

"Goddamn, why can't people learn to give correct directions?" Mark muttered.

By this time he was thirsty and hungry. It was after one o'clock and we had been on our quest since eleven.

"Shall we go home and have lunch and then start out again?" I asked.

"No, goddamn it! We are going to register now or never."

"Well, maybe we had better go back to the place in the road where it forked."

"Maybe, but Mrs. Johnson said definitely to go past the Asbury church," he reminded me.

"I know, but she might have been mistaken."

So we went back to the place where the road forked; then took the left fork. All this time we were looking for someone from whom we could get clearer directions, but we didn't see a soul until on this left fork we overtook a car, driven by a woman who not only knew where Mr. Burns lived, but offered to lead us there. She turned around, Mark and I doing likewise, and took that same long dirt road we had first taken. And, lo and behold, if she didn't stop in front of that same wood house, painted white.

"Are you sure this is it?" I called out to her.

"Yes, I'm sure."

Thanking her, we went up the driveway to the back of the house, that appearing to be the most used entrance.

"Goddamn it!" Mark exploded, "the house is brick; only that wing in the front, which must have been added on when Mrs. Johnson wasn't looking, is wood. S-s-s-s."

He suggested that I go in and find out if we had come to the right place. I rang the bell and in a few minutes the door was opened by a large, uncorseted old woman who exclaimed ecstatically, "Look who's here!"

I was taken aback. Away back. I was almost sure I had never seen this old woman before. Gulping, I managed to get out, "Is this the residence of Mr. Burns who registers voters?"

"Yes, indeedy. You come right in. I'm mighty pleased to see you."

With hesitancy, I stepped inside. Where had I known this woman? I certainly must have met her somewhere and experienced great rapport or else she wouldn't be so thrilled to see me. . . . Why was I so feeble-minded? I not only didn't remember her name, I couldn't remember ever having seen her face before.

Screwing up my courage, I quavered, "You really know me?"

"No, not that I know of."

"Oh, I'm so relieved," I gasped, "for I don't know you either; but you greeted me so warmly I thought surely you had known and loved me forever."

Her laughter cackled out and her loose body shook. "My greeting you like that don't mean a thing. I greet everybody like that."

I then explained the reason for my coming and learned that Mark and I had done wrong once again. Though it was Mr. Burns's residence and she was the mother of Mr. Burns, he wasn't registering voters there this year. He was three or four miles farther down that paved road off which we had turned, in a little unoccupied house he had rented for the day.

For the fourth time we drove along that dusty road; then turned to the left on the paved road and drove on, looking for the small, unoccupied house. Once we saw a man planting a tree by a cement bird bath in the middle of a lawn, and stopped and asked if he knew the whereabouts of Mr. Burns. "No," he answered, "I'm a stranger here."

"He must be Johnny Appleseed," Mark commented bitterly.

Reaching the crest of a long hill, we came upon an unpainted shack on the left, with one car and one motorcycle parked behind it. "Maybe that's it," I suggested.

We parked and a man we had not even seen, standing by an open well on the opposite side of the road, yelled to us that if we had come to register we were at the right place. "Step over here, please," he said, beckoning us with a big swoop of his arm.

We stepped over and the man introduced himself as Mr. Burns and we introduced ourselves and we shook hands. Then Mr. Burns waved toward a yellow scratch pad and pencil on the shelf of the "casement" that boxed in the well and invited us to sign our names.

"Don't you have a book for us to register in?" asked Mark, eying suspiciously the flimsy pad.

"Yes, but all you have to do now is write on the pad and tonight I'll transfer your names into the book."

"But we had rather write our names in the book ourselves," Mark insisted.

"Okay," Mr. Burns agreed pleasantly. He sauntered leisurely over to a nearby truck parked in a cluster of little pines and scrub oaks, lifted out from the cab a big gray ledger, sauntered leisurely back, and spread it open on the well's shelf to two pristine-white pages. Dangling from it by a cord was a stub of a pencil.

Summoning up all the dignity befitting the solemn act of becoming a voting citizen of one's newly adopted state, I picked up the pencil and wrote slowly and legibly—for once—my name at the top of the page. Then, without turning around, I moved back, treading upon a bony hound dog lying in the sand who yelped indignantly, and stood, silent and erect, as Mark signed. Even so, I felt a great deal was missing from the picture. After all our struggle, at least a band should have been playing; but all I heard was the soft wind drawing its bow across the needle strings of the surrounding pines.

11

Now that Mark and I are no longer pushed for time, we have become fairly interested in watching birds. We feel it is The Thing to do—doesn't everyone who retires watch birds? We've succumbed to the point of hanging a bird feeder on the limb of a cedar outside the kitchen window and of buying a bird book, *A Field Guide to the Birds,* by Roger Tory Peterson.

On those no-Lucille weekends when we eat our breakfast at the kitchen counter, unfortunately overlooking the sink a third full of dirty glasses and dishes left from the evening before, we keep our eyes averted to the feeder. So far we are in no danger of being smothered by birds as are our friends, the Neil Luxons in Chapel Hill, but we do have on winter mornings a respectable gathering of chickadees; grosbeaks (so we think); bluebirds or blue jays (we don't quite know the difference); juncos—those tiny, slate-colored birds that flit about as swiftly as hummingbirds—and sparrows.

As you see, we haven't yet got to be experts, but we are working at it. We used to listen when we were in the car at the right time to the Bird Watchers' radio program conducted by Charlie Gaddy on WPTF in Raleigh-Durham until Mr. Gaddy was summoned to greener fields. One afternoon we heard a lady bird watcher inquiring of Mr. Gaddy if he thought she had a yellow-shafted flicker flitting about in her back yard.

"Does he have a little black mustache?" Charlie asked.

"I haven't noticed," the bird watcher answered.

"Well, does he have black on his breast?"

"I believe so."

"Will he run a dog from a tree?"

"I haven't seen it run a dog from a tree yet."

For several weighty seconds Charlie Gaddy studied the evidence in silence; then he handed down his decision. "Well, ma'm, I wouldn't be surprised if you didn't have a little blue heron."

"Oh, thank you, Charlie," happily caroled the bird watcher.

Mark and I also try to improve our bird knowledge by reading religiously the columns on birds that appear regularly in the Sunday *Raleigh News and Observer*. Judging from the amount of space allotted to these columns, our feathered friends are "in" in a big way in North Carolina. (Another sign that they are "in" are the countless bird sanctuaries plastering the state. Once when our daughter Georgia was on her way from Pittsburgh to visit Shug and Bud, she called long distance and pleaded plaintively, "How in hell do I get out of a bird sanctuary and get into Sanford?" The *News and Observer*'s city editor himself, Jack Aulis, writes one column and another gentleman (he has to be a gentleman, don't you think, to care so fervently for the birds?), Bugs Barringer, does a column headed (please forgive him) *Bugs in the Garden*. Bugs's interests also include flowers, shrubs, and trees.

These columnists and the former participants of the Bird Watchers program go to the most amazing lengths to feed their on-the-wing guests. I can understand why Mark's and my motel is not rated AAA. All that we do when we think of it is to throw out bread crumbs from the kitchen counters; or left-over cold hominy grits mixed with bacon grease; or rotting pears and wild-bird seeds.

But these bird lovers in North Carolina outdo even Julia Childs in whipping up mouth-watering delicacies. They make pies, mind you, for the chickadees, whom, by the way, Mr. Aulis insists should by called by their original name, "towhees," (the "h" is silent, as in "Ollywood") because that is what they say. "Calling towhees 'chickadees' makes as much sense," he argues, as yelling, 'Hey, Charlie' at a guy whose name is Alden.

"Towhees also have a song," continues Mr. Aulis, "said, by those who say such things, to sound like, 'Drink your teeeeeee.' And the experts say towhees in the South have a distinct Southern drawl. I don't know what that means exactly, but I suppose the Southern towhee's song must sound like 'Drink your teeeeeee, y'all.'"

But to return to the chickadee pie: "The recipe we use," writes Mr. Barringer, "calls for one part grease (bacon), one part sugar, one part water, plus enough yellow corn meal to make it semisolid. Use a big bowl and mix it together. You can add some wild-bird-seed mixture. Almost forgot to mention to dissolve the sugar in warm water. Add bread scraps, raisins, bits of old cheese, and about anything else you might have in the kitchen."

I can't wait to try it when I have a whole week with nothing to do.

Not only do chickadees like this dish, but Mr. Barringer says it is a favorite pie of the Baltimore orioles; he puts the sugar in especially for them. When the weather gets warm and the orioles leave for the north, he advises dispensing with the sugar. (I've certainly got to remember this in case

Mark and I are ever honored with an oriole stopping over with us for the winter.)

Sparrows are also fond of it, Mr. Barringer informs his readers, and to keep them from devouring all of it, his daughter coats sweet-gum balls, after winding string around them, with the mixture. These he and his daughter "dangle from various limbs."

Though I'm still to make my first chickadee pie, I did once spend half a day spreading chunky peanut butter on pine cones (and I want you to know this is not easy) and dangling them, just like the Barringers, "from various limbs." However, for some mysterious reason, they weren't a howling—or, should I say, chirping?—success. Next time I'll mix blackberry jam, Mark's favorite, with the peanut butter.

Despite Mark's and my poor bill of fare, we are visited by a goodly number of chickadees and we delight in watching them scratch for crumbs or worms or bugs in the pine needles for, believe it or not, they scratch with both feet at the same time without losing their balance. They would make terrific ballet dancers if the feathered world ever goes in for culture. But though we watch them intently, neither of us has ever got close enough to them to tell the color of their eyes. Mr. Aulis claims with a straight face that a chickadee "comes with red eyes or white eyes." Can you imagine? "The Eastern (Northern) towhee has red eyes," he writes. "The South Atlantic towhee has white eyes. Since both mingle in North Carolina, especially in the winter, the idea of a towhee with one red eye and one white is not altogether impossible." Maybe not impossible, but scary, I'd say, especially after a late party the night before.

Quails too are quite numerous in our woods. We don't see them often, but frequently, for hours, we hear their insistent, over-and-over, up-the-scale call, "Bob*white*, bob*white*, bob*white*."

The cardinal, however, is our favorite bird, just as it's the favorite of most Tar Heels. In fact, it is the official state bird. (And mentioning that the cardinal is the state bird forces me to mention that the bee is North Carolina's official state insect. It was elected to that place of honor by no less a body than the General Assembly in its last session. A lady senator, Mrs. Bette Wilkie, Republican of Henderson, introduced the bill in the Senate and it passed without a dissenting vote. However, one senator, Mr. I. C. Crawford, Democrat of Buncombe, did rise to pose a question before the passage.

("This is a serious question," said Senator Buncombe. "Why not call it the state bee instead of the state insect? Some insects don't have a very high standing in the community."

("The North Carolina bee?" repeated Mrs. Wilkie thoughtfully, her head tilted slightly to one side. Then she firmly rejected the suggestion. "It would still be an insect," said she.

(From the Senate the bill went to the House, where it also passed with flying wings.

(And thus was the bee added to a distinguished list of official state items: the gray squirrel, the state mammal; the dogwood, the state flower; and the Scotch bonnet, the state shell.)

But speaking of the cardinal, as I was before I interrupted myself: Quite early one cold morning, I was waked up by a continuous tapping, like water dripping in the bathtub, and got up to investigate. Nothing was wrong in the bathroom but, continuing to the living room, I saw this cardinal, red as a Christmas ball, diving repeatedly at one of the big windows, his sharp bill making the tapping sound as it struck the glass. I called Mark excitedly and we stared in utter astonishment at this little ball of brilliant flame licking up the window.

Before this we had had several birds break their necks flying at night into the glass of the front windows that were illuminated from the hall lights; but never had we seen one dive again and again at a window with no apparent injury. Following the head almost simultaneously were his feet, pine-straw thin, clawing for a foothold. With feet, head, and wings in frantic action, he would flutter to the top of the window, then slip back down to the sill and ski up again. He'd repeat this performance in quick succession at least a dozen times before retiring to a bare limb of a close-by oak to recuperate, his little black eyes never leaving the shining sheet of glass.

"He must see a reflection of himself," Mark suggested, "and think it's another cardinal."

"But why would he be so mad to reach another male?" I argued.

"Maybe he's a homo."

Just in case Mark was right, I slid the big window open and threw out on the catwalk several handsful of sun-flower seed, realizing that one's mind can be diverted from sex by food almost any day or night; but our feathered friend ignored the seed completely. He even ignored a com-bination of delectable (to a bird) tidbits fashioned into the shape of a bell that had been given us as a Christmas pres-ent by Preacher and John Davenport and now swung from a limb of the same oak on which he took his time-outs.

He was interested in nothing except whatever it was he imagined he saw in the glass.

"Perhaps he has a Narcissus complex," suggested a friend who dropped in. "You know, just crazy about himself."

"Well, I don't know for sure about that," Mark said, "but

I do know he's crazy, absolutely crazy, and that's one thing we don't need around this house—another crazy thing."

All day long he bombarded the window; only when night came did he desist. And all the next day, and the next day, and the next day. . . . When Mark and I waked up in the mornings, we would listen first thing for that tapping. "He's still there," one of us would say sadly.

Now and then he'd switch his attack to the window above the chimneyless fireplace. I'd enter the living room to find him standing on the outward curve of the steel hull that housed the fireplace, peering inside, his little head tilted slightly to one side. In time the top of the hull became whitish-gray with his droppings, as did the sills of the window.

"I'd batter him to death if I could get a hold of him," Lucille threatened, standing in the middle of the living room, her baseball-mitt-sized hands clenched on her big hips.

Appalled, I asked, "You mean you'd kill him?"

"Yas'm, I sho would. He don't do nothing but mess up my windows."

"But he's such a beautiful bird."

"Not to me he ain't."

After ten days or more had passed, he was joined by a female cardinal. She perched close to him on the oak limb or on the rail of the catwalk that he had begun to occupy occasionally during his rest periods, singing madly what we trusted was: "Won't you come home, Bill Bailey; won't you please come home?" But he wouldn't go home, so after a week, disheartened, as we could plainly see, she departed, never to return.

"It looks as if he'd be exhausted," Mark remarked one day, eying him as he skied up the window for the millionth time.

And no doubt he was, for the next month he didn't seem so enthusiastic as at the beginning. His time-outs got longer and longer and finally, with the coming of summer, he gave up and flew away.

Until this peculiar-acting cardinal showed up, we had one other cardinal couple—at least, in our bourgeois fashion we liked to think of them as a couple. The male comes swinging down through the pine boles as swiftly as the speed of sound. He is as brilliantly red as our erotic visitor and oh, so cocky! Every time his dear little wife, robed in somber grayish brown, lights nearby, he rushes at her, snapping, I'm sure, "Woman, be gone! The nerve of you putting in your appearance when I'm here!" Mark calls him "Bully Boy" and, as I can see, admires him extravagantly.

Mark and I also find exciting the ducks that land on the river flying from north to south in the fall and vice versa in the spring and the extremely long-legged, gray-feathered cranes who travel the hundred and fifty miles from the Atlantic to stand on one foot—that is, one foot to a bird—the other angled beneath their breast, in the shallows of Rocky to peck at insects or little fish or whatever abides there. They always come one pair at a time.

Then there are the buzzards, black as midnight, who seemingly sail without stirring a feather high against the bright sky, then swoop, their great wings still motionless, just above the treetops, frequently passing between Mark and me, when we are sitting on the deck, and the ground. Sometimes for hours they circle over the same spot, having no doubt smelled a long-dead animal; then suddenly, their meal sighted, they swoop down. It intrigues Mark and me to see how, in spite of their size, they gracefully glide like kites on the currents of the air.

Now I know turtles aren't birds, but while I'm on the sub-

ject of watching, I feel moved to mention that we also watch
the turtles that sun on the rocks at the bend of the river.
As big around as automobile wheels, the turtles, hour after
hour, remain motionless, only sliding off their platforms to
swim with surprising swiftness to what must seem to them
a sunnier spot. At one time we counted more than forty.
I don't like them particularly; in truth, I dislike them vehe-
mently when I see one slither off his perch to snap at the leg
of a baby duck swimming by and drag it beneath the water.
I'd shoot them all and make turtle soup if I knew how to
pry off their armor and get to the meat inside.

In order to watch the birds and turtles better, Mark asked
me one Christmas to give him a pair of binoculars and this
request engendered one of the most heartwarming experiences of my life. It so happened that a few days after he
made the request, the Ford Foundation, of which he had
been a trustee until age necessitated his retirement, invited
us to New York for the unveiling of their fine new building
on Forty-Third Street and for a dinner at River House the
night before.

Driving to the dinner in a long, black limousine the Foundation had sent to "fetch" us, I asked Mark the names of the
trustees who had been elected to the Foundation since his
retirement. You see, I wanted to be right on my toes, calling
the new members by their correct names instead of saying
all evening, "You, sir." One introduction is never enough for
me. He told me three names and one of them I remembered:
Dr. Edmund Land, the inventor of the famous Polaroid
camera.

During the cocktail hour, as my lucky stars willed it, I
found myself having a martini with Dr. Land, of all people,
and the wife of one of the other trustees whose name I
didn't know then and still don't. After some small talk I told
Dr. Land that I was especially pleased to meet him, not

only because he was one of the world's greatest scientists, but because I felt sure he could advise me in a personal matter. Mark, I explained, wanted a pair of binoculars for Christmas and I hoped that he (Dr. Land) could tell me where to go buy them and what kind to buy.

"Mrs. Ethridge," he said immediately, "I'll send you a pair of binoculars for Mr. Ethridge."

"Oh, Dr. Land, you mustn't do that," I protested. "I wasn't hinting for a pair of binoculars [and I truly was not]; I simply wanted some advice."

"I know that; nevertheless, I'll send you a pair."

"You mustn't," I started to demur mildly again, but stopped in mid-speech when I heard loud breathing and bosom-seething beside me. It was the other trustee's wife, who was in a mighty rage because she hadn't said *her* husband wanted a pair of binoculars for Christmas. I realized if I was to save my eyes from being plucked from their sockets I must protest harder and so I did; but dear Dr. Land refused to withdraw his offer.

He did say, though, if I felt so strongly about the matter, I could send him one of my books autographed.

I decided not to mention to Mark this proffered gift of Dr. Land's. For one thing, I was sure he would accuse me of cadging, but more important, I was afraid Dr. Land might forget; I had been burned by martini promises before. And as the days passed with no binoculars appearing, I thought how smart I had been to keep my mouth shut.

But then, on Christmas eve, when I returned home from Sanford, where I had been doing some last-minute shopping, Mark asked, "What's all this about binoculars from Dr. Land of the Polaroid Company?"

"I don't know what you're talking about," I stalled, trying to look ignorant.

"Hell, you know perfectly well what I'm talking about.

While you were gone a man called up and asked to speak to you and when I said you weren't here but I'd be glad to take the message, he said he was Dr. Land's assistant and that Dr. Land wanted you to know the binoculars were on the way, air-mail express, special delivery."

"And what did you say?" I asked.

"I said, 'I presume C.O.D.?'"

"You did not."

"I most certainly did. Why shouldn't I have? Most things that come to this house come C.O.D. I didn't want to be caught without enough money, especially if you had ordered something from Dr. Land."

"Well, what did the man say when you asked him if it was C.O.D.?"

"He said—pretty snootily I thought—'Not likely, Mr. Ethridge.'"

When the package arrived—guess what? There were two pairs of binoculars, his and hers!

Some people said I should send Dr. Land two books in return, but I argued if he had wanted two, he would have said two. I'm not one to give my books away freely. But which book to send him? Which would interest him most? Pondering this, I remembered that in my book *Russian Duet*, which was the account of the trip I made to Russia in 1958 with my friend Nila Magidoff, I had told how a young Wall Street broker, also visiting there, had fascinated the Russians with his Polaroid camera. How amazingly forethoughted I had been! Immediately I sent off a copy of *Russian Duet* with the notation, "See Page 181."

12

There is a snake or so, I must confess, in our Garden of Eden. Not just real snakes, though they are bad enough; but other nuisances that might be termed "snakes in the grass."

Every now and then, Mark and I glimpse a black snake slithering slowly across the road, and once on a May day close to the river, with a half-dozen guests in my wake, I came upon two water moccasins. I was smugly leading this little group through the laurel garden, which was wearing on every satiny green shoulder and bosom a loosely knotted, round corsage of fragile, faintly pink flowers, when suddenly, directly in the path, a foot or more away, were these two snakes—one coiling down from the branch of a tree and one coiling up from the ground, just like those cobras you've seen in movies writhing to music out of the baskets of Indian fakirs. Their long, flat heads were just a few inches apart.

I screamed and jumped back quickly, scattering to the rear all those behind me except one heroic gentleman, Ed Yaggy, of Chapel Hill, who instantly picked up a rock and flung it at the snake on the ground. Whether he struck it none of us could see, for both moccasins disappeared into the underbrush as smoothly and suddenly as lightning into the sky.

Regrouping, my friends and I went shakily and silently on until Ed, with laughter sputtering over every word,

103 ಕ್

asked, "What do you know about us interrupting an act of copulation?"

That amused and somewhat relaxed us all. It also bemused me. Did snakes really copulate? And if they did, how did they? On the surface of things, it didn't seem possible, but then, I'm woefully ignorant in the matters of sex. Once, Bud overhearing me make a stupid remark on the subject, exclaimed, "Willie, you're so ignorant about sex, I don't understand how you managed to have four children."

"I understand perfectly how I had four children," I answered promptly. "What I don't understand is why in my forty-nine years of marriage I didn't have forty-nine."

So, this day of the two snakes, I kept my mouth shut and very shortly led my little band back to the house. I could see they had lost all interest in the laurel, corsage-bedecked though it was like the officers at a convention of the D.A.R.

These two are the only poisonous snakes I've seen on The Land, but Georgia and Sefton Abbott have declared several times in the wildest frenzy that they, while swimming in the river, have seen them. One day they reported they had even seen one with a fish in its mouth.

Besides snakes, we have rabbits, countless cottontail rabbits, who happily eat up the violets I so painstakingly plant faster than I can plant them. Long, long ago in the thirties, when I visited the Martha Berry School in North Georgia and saw violets bordering all the paths through the woods, I determined right then and there that if I ever had a place in the deep country, I, too, would have violets edging the walks. And I'm working diligently at it, but these rabbits, I hate to admit it, are more agile then I and are doing their best to thwart me.

"Darn it, there must be thousands of them," I mourned to Mark one day and, as I found out later, I wasn't exaggerating one whit. I read in a book—and it has to be so since I read it in a book—that Chatham County has been "blessed [that's the author's exact word] from the beginning with an abundance of cottontail rabbits. . . . Eventually, farmers, and especially farm boys, found that rabbits could be marketed at eight to fifteen cents each. So trapping of rabbits became a big business in Chatham. . . . With the development of rail transportation, rabbits were shipped to out-of-county and out-of-state markets. Travelers found 'Chatham Rabbit' on the menus of New York hotels. . . . These rabbits were packed in light barrels, with the cold November to January temperature serving as natural refrigeration. Chatham became the number one rabbit county in the state, and this association persisted until displaced by the broiler-producing title."

An out-of-the-county minister, so I also read, once held a series of meetings for a week in Chatham and had rabbit served him in every conceivable form, so at the final meal he offered this grace:

"O Lord, we have had rabbits warm, and we have had rabbits cold. We have had rabbits young and we have had rabbits old. We have had rabbits tender, and we have had rabbits tough. We thank Thee, Lord; we have had rabbits enough."

The author's assertion that "the broiler" usurped the rabbit's number-one title in the county sounds reasonable to me. Though we have no chickens on The Land, they are on practically every other acre of the county. Riding along the country roads, you see many low, long, unpainted, but softly weathered chicken "houses" and processing plants sprawled in the woods. I bought a whole ton of chicken droppings from one close by to fertilize our rocky ground, which was a stroke of good fortune; but on the other hand,

I and other gardeners find getting male help very difficult, for so many men in the county spend their days and nights "plucking" chickens. It is a big business and pays well.

However, a tremendous number of chickens are shipped unplucked. The traffic between Pittsboro and Chapel Hill and destinations much farther north is frequently slowed to a truck's pace by pyramidoidal loads of slatted coops stuffed with squawking leghorns while the air behind them is snowflaked with white, fluttering feathers. Now and then a frantic squawker squeezes through the slats and hurtles to the roadside, landing, alas, dazed or dead, to be picked up by a following motorist. I have seen on one trip as many as four dead white leghorns on the roadside between The Land and Chapel Hill.

Besides snakes and rabbits and chickens, we have wasps and tiny little gnats you can't even see, only feel. The wasps build their nests along the rims of the windows and doors of the loggia and the catwalk. We spend practically all of our social security checks on sprays to annihilate the wasps so that we can scrape down their nests in safety.

The gnats are much worse. They don't build anything I know of; they just bite—quick, stinging, itching, needle-sharp bites. We aren't infested with them often, thank God. They seem to come out of the nether regions only when the air is hot, still, and muggy. They simply adore my eyes, insignificant as my eyes are. Usually when I discover they are about, I put on close-fitting, dark glasses; but on those days that I forget, I'm likely to be stabbed. And always on an eyelid. And always my eyelid swells up to three and four times its ordinary thickness. Though I'm allergic to only one other thing as far as I know—Coricidin—I'm terribly allergic to whatever it is this mite of a gnat shoots me with.

One afternoon my eyelid was so swollen and my eye so

inflamed I hesitated to go to a cocktail party to which Mark and I were invited. "I hate to go to a party looking like this," I said to Mark.

"Don't be childish," he retorted brusquely. "Who in the hell do you think is going to look at you?"

Then in warm weather there are chiggers that bore under the skin and cause it to redden and hump up and itch much worse than going-away measles. When I go into the woods to work in the summer I put sulphur, which for some God-given reason they don't like, in my shoes and garden gloves and when I come in I quickly take a steaming hot bath and scrub with the strongest soap I can find. Old-fashioned Octagon would be best, but I can't find any in these parts. If the chiggers do bore in on me, I paint the lumps with nail polish; it is supposed to smother the creatures and sometimes it does.

Bud says the only remedy is to get in a tub of kerosene, immerse oneself completely and then ignite the kerosene. He's terribly allergic to them; once he was so badly infested, he had to take cortisone. And, oh dear Lord, the areas of the body they feast upon are those most tender and sensitive, such as under the arms, in the crotch, and in the "canal" that separates the buttocks.

We also have moles. I despise them worse than snakes. All summer, day and night, night and day, they crisscross beneath the lawn, humping it up as if it were whiplashed. And, of course, all the grass on the pushed-up ridges dies, for the roots are exposed to the air. Early every morning I tap dance as madly as a teen-ager, struggling to stomp the ground back in place; nevertheless, there are brown streaks zigzagging like needlework across a green background.

As tormenting as the moles is the garden hose. Now, I know hose is an inanimate object; still, did you know one

107 ෬෯

end of a hose is called "she" and the other end "he" and if you try to join a "she" end to another "she" end you are in trouble, serious trouble? In fact, it can't be done. Before I got this baffling fact through my head, I tried unsuccessfully many, many times to do it. But that isn't all that's demoniacal about hose. It resents being moved. Just try to pull a mile of hose along an open path or road or even across a lawn and you'll see what I mean. It can find a dozen rocks or roots or dwarf bushes to grab on to and never, never turn loose. You can jiggle and wiggle and slam the hose about, but in the end you have to retrace your weary steps until you reach the wee, unnoticed impediment, bend your aching back, and lift up the hose. And if a hose can't find anything—not any little measly thing—to clutch to, it will tie itself into a tight knot, a knot that demands you pull the end of the hose farthest from the knot all the way back and worm it over and under and around until you drop dead. No, indeed, no one can make me believe hose isn't animal; the most contrary animal there is.

As I said, Mark's and my Garden of Eden isn't perfect; but even so, it is more perfect than we deserve.

13

Just when we were beginning to feel at home in North Carolina and were congratulating ourselves on our decision to settle there to be near two sets of our children and grandchildren, David informed us that he and Eleanor and the three little boys (yes, I know I said in the beginning they had one, David; but another, whom they named Nathaniel, arrived shortly after we moved, and two years later they had a third, whom they named—of all names we didn't need—Mark, making him Mark V) were moving to Steamboat Springs, Colorado.

They had not only been a source of great joy to us since we came to North Carolina, but, I must admit, of considerable anxiety too.

Hardly a day passed that one of the boys wasn't in trouble. They did everything they weren't supposed to do except smoke marijuana. Eleanor is the most conscientious, loving, and gentle of mothers, but she is a mite absent-minded and vague. The children would escape from her sight when she was daydreaming or busy and do themselves in or get done in by others. They got in the medicine cabinet and ate too many aspirin or drank too much hair spray or shoe polish and had to be rushed to the emergency room of the North Carolina Memorial Hospital to have their stomachs pumped out.

On one occasion, Nathaniel, aged five going on six, who

109 ०꒰

had been tucked in his bed for his afternoon nap, crawled out the window and "flew," so he proclaimed, "to the moon and walked all about." Unfortunately, however, this "giant step" ended in a manhole from which he, screaming bloody murder, was rescued by a passer-by. Another day he sneaked into the station wagon Eleanor had left parked on the top of a steep grade, released the brake, and went hurtling down the hill a hundred feet or more to a big lake and was saved from drowning only when the station wagon swerved at the last minute into a tree. Nails in feet, contact glasses (Eleanor's) in stomachs, and knife gashes in fingers, arms, and legs were common occurrences. In fact, dear Eleanor dashed so frequently to the emergency room she was stricken with embarrassment to the point that once she tried to get away with a fictitious name at the admissions desk.

Mark V, who is not quite three, was the most recent emergency. He ran a horrid splinter so deeply into his foot Eleanor was afraid to pull it out herself, so once more sped to the hospital. The intern on duty was most solicitous. He put Mark V on a stretcher and gently worked at the splinter while Eleanor held Mark's head against her cheek to comfort him and still his screams. In a few minutes the splinter was out but, alas, the intern's work wasn't finished. When Eleanor tried to lift her head from Mark's, she couldn't do it. Her cheek was stuck fast to his with a thick spread of bubble gum. The intern had to soak their cheeks with ether before he could pull them apart.

Even the day of their departure for Colorado had overtones of calamity mixed with notes of absurdity. As Eleanor (David had gone on ahead) was delayed in Chapel Hill by one thing and another until she barely had time, driving long days and parts of nights, to reach Steamboat to enroll the children in school September 1, Mark and I thought we could be of the most help by seeing that the boys had the proper clothes for the first difficult days in their new surroundings. We would take them to Sanford, we decided, and fit them out from head to toe with shirts, shorts, slacks, underwear, socks, and shoes.

We went to Belk's, Sanford's largest department store. It was full of mamas and papas and children with the same objective as Mark and I and the clerks were very busy. In the confusion of getting David outfitted, Nathaniel disappeared. Nowhere could he be found; not behind counters, store dummies, in the elevators, on the stairs. Nowhere. I went up and down the aisles, yelling, "Na-than-i-el, Na-than-i-el." The whole first floor rang with "Na-than-i-el"; then the second floor; and, finally, the basement. But all in vain.

Figuring he must have gone out of Belk's, I left Mark with the other two children and took to the street. Still no Nathaniel. Then I went into Rose's and Mack's, the nearest emporiums Sanford has to what we still absurdly call "Five and Ten Cent" stores. I traipsed up and down their whirring, glittering, candy-and-popcorn-smelling aisles. No results.

A bit panicky by this time—for Nathaniel was an exceedingly beautiful and attractive five-year-old whom anybody in his right mind would covet (you understand, of course, that I'm not biased)—I returned to Belk's. Right inside the front door Mark greeted me with the news that Nathaniel had been found in a bin beneath a counter. He had crawled in and pulled closed the sliding door.

With David's and Nathaniel's trousseaux completed, my Mark, who had become mighty bored with the proceedings, suggested that while I outfitted little Mark he would take the two older boys to the barbershop and have their hair cut. They, thank God, had not yet reached the long-hair stage and didn't mind having their locks shorn. Mark said he wouldn't bother with the station wagon; he would leave it in Belk's parking lot and when I was through shopping I could pick him up.

At last I was finished, except for shoes for Little Mark. Belk had no shoes in his size, which was a blow, for he had no shoes at all. He was barefoot, just as he had been all summer. He and I would have to go to a shoe store a long, long block away. Since the shoe store was near the barbershop, I decided to drive there, and then pick up Mark and the other children. However, when I got to the parking lot there were no keys in the station wagon nor at the attendant's booth. Mark had gone off with them. There was nothing for Baby Mark and me to do except walk to the barbershop and get them; but alas, when we reached the barbershop Mark wasn't there. Nor had he been there.

"But he always comes here to have his hair cut," I argued with the barber.

"Well, yes, he does come here sometimes," he answered coldly, "but today he must have gone to some other shop."

His indifference was so chilling I didn't have the courage to ask him to let me use his phone to call one by one the other shops. Instead, dragging little Mark V behind me, I trudged to the shoe shop.

While Mark V was being fitted with shoes, I began at the top of the list of barbershops in the Yellow Pages to inquire after my erring mate. After just two calls I located him in a shop I had never heard of before. It was closer to Belk's, he said, than his regular one and he had told me very plainly before he had left me that he was going there, but, as usual, I hadn't listened. "You must learn to listen," he lectured. "You never do listen to what anybody is saying. . . ." He did agree, though, to get the car and come for his namesake and me.

Then I turned my attention to the shoe-fitting routine. To my surprise the clerk was perched on a stool he had shoved practically into the middle of the floor and was leaning far over, his head averted to one side, shoving a shoe on my grandchild's foot. The shoe looked to me to be much too big; it just swallowed the foot; nevertheless, without a moment's consideration, the clerk shoved on the other shoe.

"That does it, young fellow," he said and jumped up and back, almost falling over himself.

"They don't look like they fit," I protested. "They seem to be several sizes too large."

"They fit well enough," the man insisted.

"But they look like gunboats on his little feet."

"His feet will grow to fit them."

"But . . ."

Little Mark, weary of this colloquy, squirmed out of the chair and started to walk around. I fell back. The smell was worse than a skunk's spray and the back of his legs dripped with yellowish-brown globs. Oh, dear Lord, why had Eleanor told me he was housebroken and sent with him only training pants?

I bolted with him to the door and out, without even paying for the shoes or asking that they be charged. And nobody, but nobody, raised a hand to stop me.

Thank God, my Mark showed up shortly. With teeth clenched, I shoved the stinking bomb into the back of the station wagon and rolled down all the windows. No air conditioning for us on the ten miles to The Land. It was better to swelter than to be asphyxiated. Even so, I threw up when I got home and had to go to bed.

14

With the coming of September, the football and social season in Sanford, the town to which Mark and I are most closely attached, goes into high gear. No matter how hot the weather—and September can be powerfully hot in North Carolina—everybody in the state stops going to the beaches for the weekend, which everybody has been doing since May, and goes instead to the football games. The highways to Chapel Hill, Durham, and Raleigh crawl with the cars of fans happily on their way to see the University of North Carolina, Duke, North Carolina State University at Raleigh, Wake Forest, and other teams play their hearts out. They are on their way by eleven o'clock at least so they will have plenty of time to find places to park, pull down the tail gates of their station wagons, down a few drinks, and consume fried chicken, potato salad, cucumber and tomato sandwiches, potato chips and brownies.

Mark and I are partial to the University of North Carolina games since Mark taught there and our daughter Georgia, after graduating from Vassar, went there for her M.A. in sociology and Mr. Big was a student—at least that's what he called himself—there for two years; but the Duke games are a close second, for Shug was graduated there. We love especially to hear the Duke rooters yell: "Get the bawl, y'all; get the bawl."

This passion for football goes for basketball too. In fact,

North Carolinians may be madder about basketball than football; it is because, I imagine, they have so many excellent teams: North Carolina, Duke, Wake Forest, North Carolina State at Raleigh, and Davidson, which seem to be playing constantly in tournaments at Charlotte, or Raleigh, or Louisville, or Madison Square Garden, or some other spot.

During one basketball season I was unfortunate enough to be in the Memorial Hospital at Chapel Hill for minor surgery and I nearly died of loneliness. It so happened that the star of the U.N.C. team was in the hospital too, in a room directly below mine, for an operation on his knee, and he was the only person who really mattered in that huge institution. The doctors, the nurses, the orderlies were beyond themselves with excitement; they could talk of nothing else. One nurse even offered to roll me in a wheelchair to the door of the patient's room so I could get a close look at him.

Though I said the social season in Sanford moved into high gear in September, I didn't mean that it dies down completely in the summer. It might suffer during the hot weather by the many absentees at the seashore, but it goes on all the time. The Sanfordians, who counting the many suburbanites number around sixteen thousand, are unusually gay-spirited, bighearted, and hospitable. They throw parties for the flimsiest reasons and they are great at "ganging up" for joint celebrations. They not only get up house-warming parties for friends who've built new houses but for friends who have added on rooms to their old ones.

One day our telephone rang and Shirley Kenton caroled in her always happy, enthusiastic voice, "Willie dear, Jack [her roommate] and I and some others are getting up a party to christen the new room Lib and O.T. Sloan have built on their house and we want you and Mark to come."

"You mean you're having a room-warming?" I asked incredulously.

Her delightful laughter gushed out. "I reckon you could call it that."

And farewell parties given by three or more couples are as common as flying planes. The honor guests don't have to be going any great distance or for any length of time, but if they're going, that's sufficient. One summer Mark and I went to Germany and Ireland for two weeks and a half-dozen people or so gave a going-away party in our honor with gifts, toasts, and, of course, drinks and food. We were back before I could get my thank-you notes written, but that didn't seem to worry anybody except me.

If a bride doesn't want to be extensively entertained, but wants to save her strength for the honeymoon, her friends band together to fling whatever kind of party she will stand still for. Frequently there are more hosts and hostesses than there are guests. When Taffy McIver, the daughter of the very beloved couple Lucy Cooper and Jim McIver, got married, seven couples gave the bridal luncheon. One guest arrived with his invitation in his breast pocket so that he could refer to it when the time came for him to say his thank-yous.

Also, on New Year's Day Sanfordians demonstrate their togetherness. Either at noon or in the evening of that first day, groups gather for a traditional New Year's dinner. They all come "bringing in the sheaves" as the Baptist hymn expresses it. One year Margaret Cobb, the wife of Jim, arrived with field peas; Preacher Davenport with her famous candied tomatoes; Ellen and Bill Staton with corn bread that Bill, our state senator no less, had baked himself. Ruth and Bo Bynum, in whose home the celebration took place that year, provided the collard greens and barbecued pork.

At many parties, the guests pitch in and help the hosts

serve. Rarely is there a hired bartender or butler on hand, and not much oftener, a caterer. Two or three male friends get behind the bars and stay there for the duration and women friends go in and out of the kitchen, replenishing shrimp and crab casseroles, thin slices of bread, old ham, and other party dishes.

The biggest social togetherness occurs every April when the Stonybrook Hunt-Racing Association holds its annual steeplechase on an estate at Southern Pines and a gang from Sanford goes as one happy family. One year one hundred and sixty-four went. Several weeks before the great event, everybody planning to attend meets at Fran's and Doug Wilkinson's, whom we refer to as "our leaders," to work out who will bring what and other such vital matters. With a considerable degree of freedom each housewife announces her contribution for the day: fried chicken, old ham, beaten biscuits, stuffed eggs, sliced tomatoes and onions, potato salad, mixed green salad, sandwiches, cakes, pies . . . , but if too many volunteer to bring the same thing, Fran steps in and suggests alternates. Then the renting of the tables and chairs to be hauled down to the racing site; and the purchasing of the paper plates, cups, forks, knives, spoons, napkins, and soft drinks (hard drinks are left to the care of each individual), and ice are discussed. Doug, who has the Sanford agency for Cadillac, Oldsmobile, and other cars, furnishes the truck to do the hauling and a young man to do the loading and unloading.

The tables are set up on the grassy, sandy aisles between the rows of automobiles that cover acres of land. The parking spaces are reserved weeks ahead so that the various groups from all over North Carolina, South Carolina, and even Virginia can be together and carry on just as if they were in their living rooms at home.

Even before the tables are spread, the cocktail hour begins and frequently lasts during the entire day's meet. To view a race, one has to weave his way through lanes of cars to the fence circling the track. Many people never make it. Not that they are inebriated, you understand; it is just more fun to roam about, greeting old friends from far places, making bets among themselves, and lounging in the folding chairs that have been spread about. If one doesn't happen to see a race, he doesn't miss much—at least in my opinion, which is biased from years of schooling in Kentucky. These Stonybrook races are "on the turf" and "over hurdles" and "over brush."

That doesn't mean the North Carolinians aren't stylishly horsey. Many of the children of our friends ride and compete in horse shows around the state, and even, now and then, in Madison Square Garden. Fox hunting is also popular. Every winter I read with envy of the fox-hunting ball in Raleigh, with its formally dressed women and its pink-coated men. A couple from nearby Pittsboro, whom I haven't met yet but intend to before another winter passes, goes to this ball and takes guests.

Balls aren't only a weakness of mine, but of particularly all of Mark's and my Sanford acquaintances. They are truly the dancingest people ever. When they go to a dance, they are out on the floor every minute the music plays. The men don't gather in knots and talk business or football or basketball or politics. They dance.

At breakfast one morning, our house guest, Joan Bingham, the lovely young widow of Worth, then of Louisville but now of New York, announced, "Willie, you're the luckiest woman I know."

Wondering whether it was because I was married to Mark or because I had four such remarkable children (I'm not biased, remember?) and four even more remarkable in-laws, or because I had fourteen unbelievably brilliant and beautiful grandchildren, I answered, "I know I am, Joan, but why do you think so?"

"Because you've moved to a place where all the men are such marvelous and enthusiastic dancers."

The Sanford men are not only enthusiastic about dancing; they are extremely conscious of and vocal about the figures of their partners. Especially are they connoisseurs of bosoms; they admire madly "full-bodied girls." Just let a woman wear a low-cut dress that shows not only the cleavage but the mounds that rise from it and immediately they go into action, peering ostentatiously over her shoulder and making audacious quips. But even the "girls" with no bosoms to mention come in for their share of comments. Bud affectionately calls one friend, who is stunning but not generously endowed in the chest region, "Itty-bitty-titty-boo." Next to bosoms, the men carry on about legs. When a "girl" wears a shirt slit up almost to her thighs, the males whistle and o-o-o-o and ah-h-h and the more daring give the skirt backward flips.

Though the women, thank goodness, aren't interested in their men friends' bosoms and legs, a goodly number of them make racy remarks. Indeed, they are a lively bunch. The most daring and amusing among them is Preacher Davenport, who got her Christian name (if she has any other than Preacher I've never heard it) because she is the daughter of a Methodist minister. Unusually tall, she rises well above Mark's head when they dance, which doesn't worry him one whit, for she dances divinely; but not knowing that the first time she danced with him, she apologized in her fashion. "Mr. Ethridge," she said demurely, "I hope you don't mind dancing with tits in your eyes."

119

Catching his shocked breath—for Mark is definitely on the prudish side—he retorted, "Preacher, you didn't learn to talk like that in any Methodist parsonage."

More warmhearted and outgoing though than risqué, these Sanfordians are great kissers. As Mark once remarked, "Sanford is the kissingest town in the world. All the women greet you with, 'How you, sugar?' and a kiss."

And this goes for the men too. Not that they kiss Mark, but they do kiss me. They kiss me when I arrive at a party and they kiss me when I leave. It's lovely.

15

Mark and I are fortunate to have chosen North Carolina for our retirement years not only because our friends are so hospitable and party-oriented, but because the people in general—that is, just nodding acquaintances—are so amazingly polite, kind, and cooperative. I was deeply touched one afternoon as I was sitting on the steps in front of the Pittsboro Library waiting for Mark to finish the grocery shopping and pick me up when an elderly, strange man passing by stopped and asked with real concern, "Are you all right?"

This is a small example, however, of the North Carolinians' concern for their fellow humans. I have had two other experiences, not to mention many lesser ones, that are far more amazing.

One day, driving west from Durham to Chapel Hill on the 15-501 by-pass, I had to cross over a two-lane highway to get to the 15-501 business route going east back toward Durham, for I was invited to a luncheon at a restaurant on that thoroughfare. Well, when I reached the two-lane highway between the by-pass and the business route, I saw a big red STOP sign so I stopped like a dutiful citizen should and looked east to my right for traffic approaching from Chapel Hill. Seeing none, I moved into the highway. And there I was instantly struck by a car coming from the west, that is to say, from the same direction I had been traveling on the by-pass. (It turned out to be the business route from Durham with which I, rather a newcomer to the area, was not familiar.) I could have been killed if I hadn't had on the seat belt, for the "attacking" car, speeding at sixty miles an hour, smashed into my station wagon just where I was sitting and practically tore the whole side off. I wasn't even bruised, or, thank goodness, was the driver of the other car.

A highway patrol car appeared like magic and in spite of my arguing logically and eloquently, the policeman gave me a ticket for "failing to yield the right of way." And then he graciously offered to take me to the luncheon, which, big person that I am, I let him do.

Soon the dreaded day for me to appear in court in Durham arrived. I was terribly nervous; I had never been a defendant in court before. I kept rehearsing what I would say to the judge, though Mark kept pleading with me to say nothing. Mark insisted the judge was terribly busy; that he had a long, full calendar of traffic cases, and that I would get off much more lightly if I just admitted immediately I was guilty of the charge. But I protested I'd rather go to jail than not to say anything. I considered beginning, "Your sweet Honor," and then explain simply but movingly how I had made such a mistake, though it wasn't really my mistake but the highway department's.

On the way to Durham, Mark, fearing I would be given a big fine or a jail sentence, stopped by his bank in Chapel Hill and drew out all the cash he had. With a surprising show of affection he said he would hate for me, the mother of his children, to spend even one night in jail if he could help it.

When my case was called, I stood up, knees quaking, and, as Mark had urged, admitted I was guilty of the charge; but then I added, "However, your Honor [I did omit the "sweet"], there were extenuating circumstances if you have the time to hear them."

"Certainly," said this dear, polite judge, and gestured to me to have a seat in the chair to his left.

As clearly as I could I explained the confusion of two highways, with a median between, running in the same direction. Attentively he listened, not seeming in the least pushed for time. Then, when I finished—hold your hats, here comes my finest hour—he asked gently, "Little lady, do you have anything more to say?"

Can you imagine? I was so astonished, I couldn't add a mumbling word, but my astonishment was nothing compared to Mark's. He confessed to me later he all but died. Whether it was because the judge called me a "little lady" or, hearing me invited to say more, he couldn't decide.

I'm sure it is not necessary for me to add that the charge against me was dismissed with no points being noted on my driver's license. Such a courteous, gentlemanly judge couldn't do less. But he did do more. Or the State Highway Department did more. I'm not sure which. The next time I drove along that section of the 15-501 by-pass, I saw in large red letters beneath the order STOP, the additional admonition, "And Look Left." I feel as if a monument has been raised to me and when I die I intend to have my ashes buried at its base.

The third example of the unusual thoughtfulness and cooperation of these North Carolinians has to do with a very personal and rather embarrassing subject—my partials. You may call them bridges or false teeth, but I prefer "partials." Now, I have all my lower teeth and all my upper front teeth—six to be exact; but in the upper back on both sides I have these little partials, which are joined together behind the front teeth. In anybody else's mouth they would never show; however, when I smile or laugh, my mouth splits practically back to my ears and they can be seen by the nosy.

One morning around 7:30 while I was in the bathroom

123 ê≈

brushing these little partials, Mark came in to relieve himself. As you can see, we have togetherness morning, noon, and night. All proceeded according to Hoyle until Mark flushed the toilet and my partials, in some bizarre fashion, sprang out of my hand, dived into the toilet bowl, and disappeared with the last sickening, sucking whirl.

"Oh, Mark!" I screamed like a woman stabbed.

"What was that—an earring?"

"An earring nothing," I wailed. "That was my partial."

At any time this would have been an appalling accident, but that morning it was particularly appalling for I was speaking in the afternoon at Peace College in Raleigh. Just how could I get up in front of an audience with my back teeth, or, rather, partials, missing? Why, every time I smiled, the gaping holes would appear on both sides of my mouth. I simply had to have those partials back by the hour of my appearance.

Now here's where the account of the cooperation and kindness of the North Carolinians begins. Though Mark insisted I was wasting my time and that the gaps didn't show anyway, I got on the phone and called the plumber in Sanford. The very minute I told him what had happened, he said, "Mrs. Ethridge, I'll be right there." And he a plumber, mind you! I also called Francis Le Clair, for the plumber I had reached wasn't the plumber who had put in the septic tank—our original plumber had had a heart attack—and I was afraid this new one wouldn't be able to locate it. I couldn't help him, for I didn't know where it was, and Mark couldn't, for if he knew we had a septic tank he kept quiet about it. Mr. Le Clair said he would come as fast as his truck could make it and he would bring his man, Monroe, with him. Then I rushed forth and alerted the off-and-on yard man who had just happened to show up that morning.

In half an hour there were four men digging up a considerable area of The Land (Mr. Le Clair didn't know exactly where the tank was either). Five diggers would have been better, but Mark refused to budge from his favorite reading chair, and I had to stay on the phone to contact my dentist in Chapel Hill the second he darkened his office door to find out if he would make me a new partial by noon. At 12:30 I was being honored with a luncheon in Raleigh given by an alumna of Peace.

When I reached the dentist on the phone, he said he had an exceedingly busy morning but for me to come on and he would see what he could do. Leaving the house without one encouraging word from the diggers, I pleaded with Mark to rush to the home of the luncheon hostess with the partial if by some miracle it was found. Not believing for a moment it would be found, he agreed pleasantly.

The dentist—now, you can't beat this for cooperation— dropped everything and by noon had me fixed up with a wobbly, fragile substitute set. Overwhelmed with gratitude, I hurried to the home of my Raleigh hostess. To my amazement, she and all her other guests were hanging out the doors and windows watching for me. They couldn't wait for me to get inside of the house to see what I looked like, for Mark had called the hostess and, instead of being smart and telling her I had left my speaking notes, had announced right out that my lost teeth had been recovered and he was on his way with them.

And he did come and so, due to the sweetness and goodness of the four diggers and Mark, I appeared on the platform at Peace with my gums solidly clothed.

Unfortunately this saga of man's humanity to man had an aftermath that all but destroys my thesis that North Carolinians are so "amazingly polite, kind and cooperative." I have to keep remembering the old adage that claims the exception proves the rule.

The very morning after I had made what I considered a sparkling, brilliant exposition on the research that went into my recently published book on John Wesley, *Strange Fires*, the *Raleigh News and Observer* came out with a two-column headline screaming HONOREE LOST HER TEETH. It was unbelievable. The story related that before I appeared as the first author of Peace's Meet-the-Author Forums, I had arrived late at a luncheon in my honor because I "had flushed" my "partial plate down the plumbing." The account even told about Mark dashing like Paul Revere, except he wasn't on any horse, from our home forty miles away to the home of the hostess to bring this plate to me just as if I couldn't have eaten without it. But the cruelest cut of all was that nowhere—but nowhere—in the story was my new book mentioned!

16

October inspires me more than any other month of the year to spend every daylight hour in the woods. The flame-bright colors of the maples (rare maples the like of which I never saw before I moved to The Land, with small dainty leaves no larger than the imprints of a chicken's foot); the sour-woods, their unruly limbs drooping with slim pendants of garnet; the blatant, blushing dogwoods; and the oaks and poplars and hickories and beeches brushed with gold call insistently to me to come out and clear from under them the life-sucking underbrush and the rampant, high brown grasses. And gladly I go.

Accompanying me until recently was a Border collie with long, silky black hair curling in marcel waves over her lean body and with big, melting brown eyes. Before she was born she was given to us by a dozen Sanford couples. It was at their warming of our new house to which they brought drinks and food and a little stuffed dog as a "stand-in" for the one they were presenting us. At that hour she was being carried along with the other members of the litter by her mama at the home of the Edwin Hubbards who were in the business of raising Border collies. The Hubbards were to let us know when the puppies were old enough to be weaned from their mama and we were to look them over and have first pick.

The Sanford donors explained that Border collies were almost as smart as humans and were unexcelled as watchdogs. In England and Scotland from whence they come they are used to herd sheep, a talent completely wasted on The Land since we haven't a sheep to our names.

When the day for the selection arrived, Mark and I, as excited as if we were having a new baby, drove to the Hubbards and quickly chose a puppy who kept jumping up against the wire fence of the pen to poke her pert nose at us. We decided to name her Miss Sanford after the friends who had given her to us. The name suited her perfectly. She was a beauty queen from the moment we saw her.

But a watchdog and an Einstein she was not. Our suspicions of her timidity and weakness for strangers were first aroused when our Georgia, whom we have begun to call Big Georgia to distinguish her from the two grandchildren named Georgia, and her husband, Marc, and their four offspring arrived at three o'clock one black-winter morning, having decided to drive through from Pittsburgh rather than spend the night on the way, and Miss Sanford, who had never laid eyes on them before, welcomed them with leaps of joy and wet, tongue-lathering kisses. She was still a puppy, Mark and I reminded each other. Wait until she got a little older; then she would show us.

And she did. She was Ferdinand the Bull reincarnated. One late afternoon Mark A. and the Abbotts' dog, Maryburger, who was one-hundred and nineteen years old and as fat and wobbly as a baby hippopotamus, and Miss Sanford were lolling about in front of the house when a red fox strolled from out of the woods into the court. And what did Miss Sanford do? She fled as fast as her legs would carry her to her sleeping quarters in the basement, leaving half-dead Maryburger to waddle forth to do battle with the visitor. Fortunately for Maryburger, the fox was as startled at coming upon civilization as Mark A., Miss Sanford, and Maryburger were at seeing him.

Miss Sanford even went berserk when it thundered. One summer day when she and I were out on the lawn, thunder sounded to the south of us and she tore madly in its direction, her long body a continuous streak of shining black; then it sounded to the north and she swept past me headed in that direction; then for a little while there was a still, still silence, but instead of her quieting down, she raced around in circles, practically biting her tail. She was like one of those racing cars at the Indianapolis Speedway on Memorial Day. On her twentieth or so lap, the thunder stirred itself again and growled in the east. Off she lit like a bullet. Sad at heart, I came into the house and said to Mark, "Miss Sanford is having a nervous breakdown."

"Impossible," he answered. "She was born with a nervous breakdown."

A shadow alarmed her almost as much as thunder. When my shadow extended some distance in front of me, she pounced upon it, barked, scratched the ground, ran away from it to see if it would go away, ran back to see if it was still there, pounced, barked, tore up the ground. . . . She never stopped until I moved into the shade.

It was not just my shadow, though, that set her wild. Trotting beside Mark and me one noon to the mailbox, she suddenly whirled in her tracks and shot back toward the house. "What the hell is the matter with her?" asked Mark.

Then we saw the shadow of a buzzard that was sailing serenely against the sky.

"If Miss Sanford could only connect the buzzard with the shadow, she might not be so excited," Mark reasoned.

But how can one explain to a dog the tie between a shadow and a substance?

On one occasion we thought she herself, without our help, might grasp the idea. Big Georgia, the grandchildren, and I were swimming in Rocky when a buzzard began to circle fairly low over our heads. With unbelievable grace, Miss Sanford leaped in one curving sweep to the top of a huge boulder bordering the river, stood seemingly on tiptoe on the farthest jetting-out point, her slender head pointed toward the buzzard.

"We're going to feel like fools when Miss Sanford flies," commented Big Georgia, sending the children and me into gales of laughter, for she did look as if at any second she was going to join the big bird.

Her timidity was only exceeded by her unteachableness. She wouldn't learn she was not supposed to make a path through the periwinkle in the patio. As fast as I planted it, she trod it down. She also slept during the daytime in the northeast corner of it, keeping the ground there bare and dusty. My friend Ruth Bynum told me if I straightened the curved ends of coat hangers and stuck them in the periwinkle, Miss Sanford would stop trotting through it, but no luck. Miss Sanford hopped over them as if she were competing in the Olympic hurdle races.

She also would not learn that rocks weren't turtles, full of eggs and succulent meat. Growling ferociously, she attacked them with both front feet and her teeth. At first Mark and I told each other she was teething and the rocks soothed her gums; but after she had a full set of teeth she still gnawed at rocks the way I gnaw at lobster claws. However, I don't make the savage noises she made and I don't use my feet. No matter how deeply a rock was embedded in the ground, she wrestled with it until she loosened it and then, if it was on a hillside she pursued it and went hurtling down to the river or a ravine, as her ancestors in Scotland must have pursued wolves.

Big Georgia didn't believe Miss Sanford thought rocks were turtles. She was positive Miss Sanford was studying for a Ph.D. in geology. Once when Big Georgia saw Miss Sanford nosing a rock into a crack in a boulder, she declared, "I never saw anyone so dedicated to her science. Look, there she goes into her chapel to concentrate."

Though Miss Sanford was a little touched in the head in so many ways, now and then she did show flashes of brilliance. Once she found my dark glasses, brought them to the house, and laid them on the mat in front of the door. She also comprehended those commands that pleased her fancy. When Mark said to her, "Go get Willie," she headed straight for me, no matter where I was in the woods, and after lunging upon me, turned and started back to Mark, casting an eye over her shoulder to see if I was following her.

When I stopped to pick up a dead branch, she stopped too; then took hold of an end of it and assisted me in hauling it to the incinerator. However, when I lugged a limb or tree trunk to the river and, with superhuman effort, flung it into the current, she immediately leaped into the water, swam to the swirling limb, clutched it between her jaws, and, wet tail wagging, returned it to me. The heavier and clumsier the piece of wood, and the farther I dragged it, the more pleased she was at retrieving it. Her whole body shook with delight, drenching me from head to foot.

She helped me saw down trees, too. The second I sat down on the ground to saw, my legs spread in front of me, Miss Sanford sped forward and hopped into my lap. This, of course, necessitated my sawing around her, which was awkward, to say the least. I pled with her, "Move, Miss Sanford, please move; do, please get up, Miss Sanford. I

131 🦢

can't saw with you in my lap." I even shoved her rump with all my strength; but she didn't budge. She just settled herself more comfortably, only moving her head back now and then to lick my face with her slobbering tongue.

Nevertheless, she meant well. Plodding toward the house in the early dusk with her by my side, my heart filled with gratitude. I never had a more devoted, faithful companion—not even Mark.

Then one terrible morning when I started out to work there was no Miss Sanford leaping up to greet me. Immediately I was apprehensive; she was always at the kitchen door, waiting. I called "Miss Sanford, Miss Sanford," but she didn't come. I rushed back inside to ask Lucille if she had seen her. She hadn't. She had put her breakfast out for her as usual at the back door, but Miss Sanford hadn't touched it. I went around to the side door of the basement that has a dirt floor and extends at a shallow depth under the front wings of the house. She was accustomed to sleeping there on an old rug, but she wasn't there. I called some more; still she didn't appear. Lucille and I consoled ourselves by surmising she was down at the river, attacking turtles. Frequently when she had made a meal of turtles, her mouth was messy with a yellow substance we took to be turtle eggs, and she had no appetite for her regular diet of Alpo.

However, when she hadn't shown up by noon, I grew truly alarmed and so did Mark. We walked up and down the highway for a considerable distance to see if her body lay beside it; we searched the woods where she and I were accustomed to work; Mark went back into the basement and flashed the flashlight far beneath the low flooring. We called the sheriff in Pittsboro, but he wasn't in the least encouraging; he said there was a lot of dog-stealing in the state. We asked Bud to advertise for her over the radio station and we even got a story about her disappearance in the *Sanford Herald*.

After ten days had passed with no word of her, Mark and I had to go away for two weeks. When we returned, Bud broke the news to us that the off-and-on yard man had found her emaciated body in the basement, up under the wing, where Mark had searched with the flashlight. The decaying smell had led to the discovery.

The yard man refused to touch her, so dear Mark Abbott came out and thoughtfully buried her in a spot in the woods where I was unaccustomed to working and wouldn't be reminded of her by the site of her grave.

But I don't need the site of her grave to remind me of her. I think of her again and again and try to fathom out why she happened to die. It is such a mystery. Mark's and my guess is that she was bitten by a moccasin or hurt by a car; and that she had lain in the woods until she could finally drag her dying body home.

17

Chatham County has as agreeable a climate as ever I came across, except for about four weeks in the summer when it gets really hot—in the low nineties, that is—and humid; and in the winter when it is plagued once or twice with ice storms. According to official figures, the "basic characteristics" of the climate are as follows:

"Average annual precipation: 44 inches

"Average January temperature: 43° F

"Average July temperature: 78° F

"Average length frost-free season: 200 days."

Scarcely, you see, any snow or freezing weather that lasts more than two or three days; just now and then these ice storms, which seal all limbs, leaves, blades of grass, wires, and roofs. The ice encases everything completely like a suit of shining armor encased a warrior of the Middle Ages. Small bushes, such as azaleas, look as if they should be ornaments for sale in the glass departments of Bonwit Teller's and Bloomingdale's. The stems inside are not even discernible and the blades of grass in the lawn stand up like fragments of stalactites.

Breathtakingly beautiful it is, to be sure, but so dangerous and destructive. The green-clothed hollies, cedars, pines, and magnolias either bow to the ground beneath their unbearable burden or tear off their limbs to get relief. Frequently the bent-over trees and dropped limbs break off electric wires and leave houses without lights, heat, and, in the case of those who depend on wells run by motors, such as Mark and me, without water.

This happened to us late in February one winter. I awakened in the early morning, as is my sprightly custom, and tried to turn on my bedside light. When it didn't come on, I thought the bulb had burned out; I, who am an optimistic soul, can never believe anything so crippling as no current can overtake me. I jumped up and tried all the lights in the bedroom, the hall, the living room, the kitchen. There was no mistake; we were without electricity. Also there was no water, not even enough to clean our teeth, and no heat to warm our shivering bones. Fortunately we cook with natural gas; but man cannot live by food alone. Mark and I hauled iced wood (we can never remember to get in wood when the weather is warm and steeped in sunshine) and built huge fires in our bedroom and the library-dining room. The temperature, however, dropped and dropped.

When bleak night skated in and no help had arrived from the Carolina Power and Light Company, Mark and I moved into Shug's and Bud's house in Sanford, where we stayed for two days and two nights until we got the word that "service" had been restored. But the hardest blow was still to come. When we reached The Land, we discovered we had lost in the glen sixteen fully grown pines, two hollies, and a huge, hoary-haired oak at least one hundred feet high and eighteen feet in circumference at its base. Heartsick, we hired three woodcutters to clear out the mess. They were able to haul out the sellable pine; but the mountains of limbs of hollies and heavy rounds of oak had to be burned in the woods as the incinerator and the river were too far away. This was scary business. Very carefully we chose the most open, accessible spot on the high rim of the ravine and cleared it of sticks, leaves, and young growth.

For five days all went well; then came the sixth day that

would finish the job. In the late afternoon, anxious to get away with their golf-winners' sized checks, the woodcutters hurriedly shoveled dirt on the incompletely burned pile of limbs and logs until it appeared to be out.

The men left and I, weary as I had never been, dragged myself into the house, soaked my aching bones for an hour in a hot tub, put on a long, fleecy nightgown and woolen robe, and watched the news on TV until 7. Then I decided to go outside and look across the wide chasm to the far ridge where the fire had been. I wanted to be absolutely sure it was out.

I quickly reached the near side of the chasm's rim and lifted my eyes to search the far side. Immediately I saw the fire. The pronounced-dead ashes had flamed into new life.

I was absolutely panicked. I had to get over immediately to that distant rim. Wildly I rushed back into the house to tell Mark and to grab up the flashlight, for the night was black as swamp ooze. I could never get down that thickly wooded, limb-strewn ravine, cross the deep stream bed, and struggle up the other side without a light.

Reaching the low brick loggia, I was so excited I forgot to lift my foot sufficiently to mount it and sprawled flat, my left knee and wrist taking the brunt of the jolt. However, the pain wasn't bad enough to stop the hammering of my heart and to prevent me from stumbling up and dashing into the house.

"The fire has rekindled!" I screamed to Mark. "Where's the flashlight?"

"On the counter in the kitchen," he called back. "Wait for me!"

"I can't wait. The woods will be on fire if I don't get there right away."

"Wait! . . ."

I grabbed the flashlight, ran outside, and tore about looking for a shovel. I was sure it wasn't in the basement where
it should be. On a recent visit I remembered that Bubber
had begun a low retaining wall to hold back from the road
the rain that fell on the gently slanting Social Circle and he
had had the shovel. But it wasn't there. I grew more panicked. Where could it be? I had to have it. There was no
way of getting water to the fire site. Dirt was the only thing
that would drown the flames. A vision of the shovel leaning
against a bush on the edge of the lawn appeared before my
frantic eyes. I sprinted in that direction. It was there. With
the heavy, awkward shovel in one hand, the flashlight in the
other, I raced for the woods.

As I was entering them, Mark came out of the house.
"Wait for me, Willie!" he yelled. "I'm coming with you!"

"No, I can't wait!" I yelled. "You're too slow."

I plunged down the steep slope, crashing through the
dead, fallen limbs we had never had the time to pick up,
the countless small maples, oaks, sourwood, ash, dogwood.
. . . I was conscious of them switching at my face and tear-
ing at my full-length gown and woolly bathrobe and bedroom slippers. I stepped calf deep into a stump hole and
was thrown to the ground.

At the bottom of the gorge, I tried to cross the yawning
stream bed on a log that extended over it, but a third of the
way over my knees got so shaky I turned around and,
shakier than ever, crept back. On my seat I slid down the
embankment, then clawed like a rat up the other side and
continued on up the ridge.

The whole round mound of supposed-to-be ashes and
smothered logs flickered with blue and yellow tongues a
foot or more high, and with cerise coals. So far the flames
were contained within the cleared circle, but how long they

would continue to be contained tormented my frightened mind. Any second they might leap into the dry, crisp leaves beyond the raked area and into the nearby pines and other trees. Then there would be no stopping them; the whole of Chatham County east of Rocky River would go up in flames.

After several tries, I lodged the flashlight on a stump to fan out over the hole the woodcutters had dug, clutched the shovel, and began to dig.

"Willie, come back!" I heard Mark crying from the far-away hilltop. "Willie, come back!" He sounded as if he had been crying that way for a long time; I had simply failed to hear him over the rustling of the stirred-up leaves and the cracking of the dead sticks beneath my feet. "Willie, come back, goddamn it! Come back right now!"

I felt a little sorry for him. I had taken the only flashlight and he could not possibly get down that rugged gulch without one. "I can't come back," I bawled, "but don't worry, I'm all right."

"Goddamn it, I said come back!" he continued to yell. "Come back I tell you!"

I desperately needed all my breath and all my strength to ram that shovel into the frozen ground, yet I had to keep bawling, "I can't come back."

The owls and other creatures of the night must have thought Mark was trying to save some straying soul from crossing the River Styx as he kept up his plea: "Come back, goddamn it, come back!"

I threw the first shovel of dirt into the pyre, but nothing happened. Nothing. I shoveled again and threw; shoveled again and threw; shoveled again and threw. Still no change. The greatest drawback was the small amount of dirt I was able to get out. Though the shovel would feel heavy as I drew it from the ground, by the time I lifted it to the surface the netting of roots in the earth had scraped out all except a handful. Also, to reach the fire I had to walk several feet where no light shone and I frequently stumbled and spilled still more.

"Willie, come back!" came the unnerving cry across the chasm. "Come back!"

"I can't, Mark." By this time I was impatient. "Can't you see I can't come back?"

"Goddamn it, come back!" he went on wailing as if he hadn't heard me, and I realized that perhaps he hadn't. His ears weren't as keen as they once were. "Come back!"

I shoved the spade deep with my foot, eased the load up, felt my way carefully forward and flung the dirt directly on top of a stump, which was winking like a lady's dinner ring with rubies of fire. Thank God, the rubies blacked out as if I had pulled a glove over them. I was much cheered, but very briefly. The glowing places sobered down only to revive by the time I returned with a new load. As if infuriated at my audacity to stifle them, they flashed out even longer spears of blue flame.

I decided the logs were piled too high, one atop the other. Crowded together, they could smolder and shoot out sparks all night. The woods would never be safe. The chunks should be pulled apart so they would be exposed and the sand would get to them. I jabbed the spade between two brightly burning logs and jogged the top one off. But, oh lawd, it didn't stop on the edge of the fire as I had expected, but kept rolling. Like a comet it somersaulted down the slope, setting fire to the leaves and bushes as it went. I was wild with fright. I would never be able to get the blazing streamer out, much less the trees that turning bomb might set.

Almost crazy, I raced behind it and overtook it as it

lodged against a stump halfway down the declivity. What to do first? Where to begin to fight? I started stamping the burning leaves with my bedroom-slippered feet and beating with the shovel. I never moved as swiftly on a dance floor. Stopping to catch my breath, I heard the big dinner bell on the catwalk ringing. Mark, evidently exhausted yelling into the unresponsive night, had retreated to the house and resorted to the bell. Let it ring, thought I. Maybe Mr. Mc-Kelvey from across the highway would hear it and, though he couldn't be of any assistance to me because of his emphysema, he might come over and keep Mark company.

The leaves finally out, I studied the guilty log. Curiously enough, it was rounded at the ends, making a perfect ball. I knew I should get it back to the fire where it could be hemmed around with cleared ground. I felt about for a sturdy stick to help me scoop it up on the shovel. Accomplishing this delicate feat, I started up the slant, only to trip in a coil of grapevine. The wooden head, with its hundreds of red, snapping eyes, tumbled off the spade and started once more down the hill.

"Willie, goddamn it, come back!" Alas, Mark had returned to the lawn and was once more bleating forth. "Come here this minute!"

Hearing him in the midst of my predicament, I flew into a rage. Lifting my head I screamed at the top of my lungs, *"Shut up!"*

It took longer this time to get the log back on the shovel, for my hand on the stick trembled so fearfully. At last, though, it teetered near the handle and I made it successfully back to the pile of flames and cinders. Then I returned to my shoveling. The earth in the hole was getting harder and the take each time smaller. My wrists and back ached. My eyes and head ached. My legs and feet ached. However,

I was making progress. I pulled aside a few more rounds of trunks, very, very carefully this time, and beat out the scarlet bugs of heat boring in them. The fire seemed out now; but to be safe, a few more shovels of sand. . . .

Suddenly I heard dogs baying excitedly to the right of me. They were all I needed to make this night complete. They were on a fresh scent, I could tell, and coming straight toward me. The Coon Hunters Club from across the river must be hunting those little animals that give the organization its name. Though our land was posted and they weren't supposed to be on it, they definitely were. And very close by, too.

I flung aside the shovel, grabbed up the flashlight, and flew as fast as my legs would carry me toward the house. I had the terrifying idea that in the dark those yelping hounds would mistake smelly, sweaty me, for a possum and tear me to pieces.

"Willie, come here!" I heard Mark still calling, even above the racket of the dogs. "Goddamn it, I tell you to come here!"

"I'm coming, Mark," I managed to answer between pants. "I'm coming, darling."

As I reached the clearing I could dimly make out Mark's figure, nattily attired in his new overcoat and the fake-fur hat the Abbott children had given him for Christmas. Staggering toward him, I anticipated his fervent embrace and comforting words of praise. "Kiddo [his most passionate nickname for me], you are the greatest," I was confident he would say. "The very greatest. I've never been so proud of anyone in my life. You are the most courageous, the most persevering, the most heroic . . ."

Instead, with no embrace, he angrily scolded: "You are the biggest goddamned fool that ever lived. You frightened

141 ॐ

the living——out of me. You know how long you've been over there at that fire? Two hours and fifteen minutes by the clock. And I was frightened to death every minute. You are the biggest goddamn fool. . . ."

I hoped Smoky the Bear loved me.

18

Our would-be-helpful water-witching neighbor, John Mc-Kelvey, took time out from planting his vegetable garden one spring morning to pay us a visit and to commiserate over our frustrating telephone service. Unfortunately Mark had gone to Sanford for his laundry and so I alone shared his suffering.

Mr. McKelvey, Mark and I, and several hundred other people have the most exclusive, expensive, exasperating phone system, The United Telephone Company of the Carolinas, Inc. Our Company is not unique to North Carolina; nor, as I understand it, to other states; but that doesn't make it any easier to swallow. In North Carolina, there are twenty-eight of these so-called "independent companies" with 695,000 subscribers out of a total in the state of 1,456,000. These "independent" companies cover fifty-five percent of the area of North Carolina and over half the area of the United States.

In our case, a telephone call to anyone who is not a subscriber of the United Telephone Company of Carolina, Inc. costs each of us a minimum of thirty-five cents for three minutes. This charge also applies to people outside the "system" who call us. Bud's and Shug's telephone bill one month was $94.00, practically all of it for calls to Mark and me just ten miles away. And our bill for that month and others are much, much more. Mark and I know only the Le

Clairs and Mr. McKelvey in our "Company," whom we can call for free.

But, alas, more serious than the cost, is the difficulty of contacting the operator. I strongly suspect our "Company" has only one operator on duty at a time. When I try to get her between nine o'clock in the morning and ten and get no response, I mutter to Mark, "She's undoubtedly gone to the little girls' room. It's her regular time to go." She suffers from no "irregularity," as those TV commercials so delicately put it. Once I grew so exhausted waiting for the operator to answer that, when she finally did, I said, "If the house had been on fire, it would have burned to the ground by now," to which she snapped, "You must remember there are other people who want to use the telephone."

"I can't imagine why," I retorted brilliantly.

Our operator is so unobliging she won't even give you the time of day. And that's no figure of speech. One morning when Mark and I waked up we realized that our two electric clocks had stopped during a lightning storm in the night and that Mark's watch, which was very untrustworthy, gave an hour that didn't seem to correspond with the height of the sun. So I called the operator and asked sweetly, "Will you tell me the time, please?"

"No," she answered flatly. "We don't give out the time."

"But I need to know," I implored. "Our clocks stopped in that electric storm last night and we have guests who have to catch a plane." Which was the truth.

"Well, in that case it's seven-thirty; but don't ask again."

Our struggles are nothing now compared to what they were the first months, when we were on the line with nine other people. That is, nine other telephones; there must have been at least ten people to each telephone. And such talkers! Shug couldn't hold a candle to them. One day before the house was quite finished, though the telephone was in, I had to call a wallpaper establishment in Southern Pines to tell the management he had sent the wrong rolls of paper for the bathroom. There stood the hard-to-get paper hanger at my elbow, brush in hand, paste drying, and no wallpaper that I had ever seen before, much less ordered. I put the phone to my ear and heard the casual, slow drawling voices of two females. I hung up and waited; then lifted the receiver again. The same two voices. I hung up and waited some more. Again the receiver to my ear. Again the unhurried voices. I went out on the catwalk that runs across the back of the house and paced up and down. Up and down. I was afraid, though, to pace too long for fear those two women might hang up and two more get on the line before I could.

At last, pushed beyond my endurance, I decided to listen in so I could put in my call the second they hung up. They were discussing, as if they had all day, the indifferent appetites of their children. "Now, Jimmy will eat a little spinach if I chop it up real good and cook it with a big plot of oleo," said one.

"Harriet won't touch spinach," said the other with a heart-tearing sigh. "She spits it out as fast as I spoon it into her mouth. But she'll eat carrots fairly well. She likes 'em raw better than cooked."

There was a long pause. Evidently the mother of Jimmy was struggling to think of something else Jimmy would eat. Nothing coming to mind, she began to name the members of her family who had shown up for dinner the past Sunday.

The mother of Harriet clucked her tongue leisurely. I could tell she was shocked at the number who came; but, recovering after a minute or two, she inquired, "What'd you have 'jeat?"

145 ॐ

Jimmy's mother listed everything: barbecued spareribs, boiled cabbage, sweet potatoes, turnip salad, rutabagas, tomato pickles, corn bread, apple pie. . . .

When she finished, there was another long silence. Definitely there was nothing more to say, but neither could bear to hang up. Finally a question came to Harriet's mind. "Do you make your corn bread with buttermilk?"

"If I have it. I think buttermilk makes the best corn bread myself."

"I think so too. There's something about buttermilk. . . ."

Wild with impatience by this time, I began to jiggle the hook up and down to alert those two creatures to my presence on the line.

"Myrtle," said one (I was in such a state I couldn't tell whether she was Harriet's or Jimmy's mother), "do you hear someone eavesdropping on us?"

"Yes," I broke in quickly, "I'm listening in and I want you to know I think it is very inconsiderate of you two to keep the phone tied up for an hour the way you have."

"And I want you to know, lady, I think it is very inconsiderate of you to interrupt our conversation. . . ."

"After an hour . . . ?"

"What do you mean, after an hour?" snapped either Harriet's or Jimmy's mother. "I looked at the clock when I got ready to call my friend and it was exactly twenty minutes to eleven."

"Well," said I tauntingly, "will you be so kind as to look at the clock now and tell me the time?"

After a moment, evidently spent scrutinizing the clock, she crowed, "It is now only eleven thirty."

"I beg your pardon," I answered silkily. "I was mistaken. You've been talking only fifty minutes instead of sixty." And with that gloating thrust I hung up.

That colloquy, I realized when I had cooled down, was no way to begin a life in a new neighborhood and I vowed to do better from then on, and I have, but it hasn't been easy. It appeared to me those months that the only recreation of the nine people on our line was telephone conversations. They talked and talked and talked as if they were spending the day together and had twelve hours to fill with words.

Mark's and my problems with a party line had long been over, but Mr. McKelvey, to hear him tell it that spring day, was still battling with fellow linesmen, or rather lineswomen, over the use of the phone.

"There I was, Mrs. Ethridge, trying to make a call before the business houses closed and these two women were yacking and yacking and yacking," he mourned. "I kept picking up the phone to dial the operator, only to discover they were still at it. About the sixth or seventh time I tried to call one of the women said, 'And then there were the Andrews sisters' . . . My God, they were getting back to ancient history. Nobody's heard of the Andrews sisters since they sang *The Money Tree.*

"I realized I had to do something so I began to click, click, click. Finally one of them said, 'Someone must want to use the phone. I suppose we'd better hang up.'"

" 'Lady,' I put in before she could change her mind. 'That's the best idea you've had today.'

"You know, Mrs. Ethridge, they think they own the line. When they can't think of anything to say, they just breathe. They can't bear to hang up the phone. They breathe while they ask themselves, 'What can I say next? Is there any news I've forgot to report? Has anybody been born? Has anybody got married? Died? Divorced? Has anybody got sick or been locked up?' Once, after one of those long breathing sessions, one party cried out triumphantly, 'Stella Louise, I ran the vacuum cleaner yesterday!' "

Dear Mr. McKelvey himself stopped a moment or two to breathe. His emphysema was causing his breath to come in and out in very short puffs. Yet his little blue eyes were as bright as ever and his fat cheeks as rosy red.

"Once, Mrs. Ethridge, I was widow-chasing over at English Springs," he began once more, "and I wanted to call the lady up, but as usual my line was busy. As you can understand, I was impatient to get through so I began to jiggle. In a few minutes one of the parties said angrily, 'I wonder who that is interfering?'

" 'I'll tell you who I am,' I snapped back. 'I'm not ashamed to tell you and I just dare you to report me!'

"What gets me, Mrs. Ethridge, is that these people come home from work where they've been together for eight hours and the first thing they do is they call one another to talk about the work they've been doing all day. Everybody on my line either works in Pittsboro at that Kaiser-Roth hosiery company where they make stockings and socks, or at the Chatham Mills, making labels, just labels. That's all that big mill does, Mrs. Ethridge, is make labels twenty-four hours a day. It certainly surprised me when I learned that. I had no idea there were so many people in the world wanting labels. . . ."

"Nor did I," I put in.

"Well, that's neither here nor there," he interrupted quickly, as if I might take over the conversation if I got a little headway. "The point I was making was that these people come home after working side by side all day and get on the phone and yack, yack, yack about the work they've been doing. The Chatham Mills workers discuss over and over which shift is the best—the shift between midnight and eight o'clock in the morning or the shift between eight o'clock and four in the afternoon or the shift from four till midnight. And the hosiery company workers want to know whether it is better to heel or to toe. Whenever I pick up the phone and hear them going back and forth, I grab my poor head and groan to myself, 'There they go—heeling and a-toeing! Now, what I want to know, Mrs. Ethridge, is why they can't argue those matters on the companies' time instead of yours and mine?"

Receiving no soothing answer from me, he recovered his home-grown and home-carved walking stick from the floor, hoisted himself out of Mark's chair, and departed, still shaking his head and softly puffing.

19

Living in the country a goodly number of miles from the nearest grocery store does have its handicaps. No matter how assiduously we keep jotting down items we are running low on, we frequently face days without butter or bread or milk or wine vinegar, or eggs, or sausage, or toilet paper, or lettuce, or bourbon, or paper napkins, or rice, or. . . . You name it; we're out of it.

When such happens, I look accusingly at Mark, since he's taken over the grocery shopping, and he looks accusingly right back, since I'm supposed to make out the list of items to be bought.

"No grapefruit," I cried out mortally wounded one morning.

"No, no grapefruit," he retorted brusquely. "There was no grapefruit on the list. If you want grapefruit, write it down. I don't keep the house."

Usually we manage to substitute a similar product for the one that's missing and don't lose a pound, but one morning we were out of luck. When Lucille appeared with our breakfast trays, she announced with considerable indignation, "There was no grapefruit, no oranges, no orange juice, no prunes, no apple sauce, no nothing, so I had to bring you peaches."

It being April, I was surprised. "Where did you find peaches?" I asked.

"In a glass jar on the shelf."

And so she had. A jar of brandied peaches I was saving to serve with ham.

These oversights have pushed me into nightmares. That is no figure of speech; it is the literal truth. One sticky, humid Saturday night I dreamed that Mark and I were having a big luncheon with hundreds of people milling about, drinking martinis and Bloody Marys, when Shug's and Bud's maid, Mabel, whom we had borrowed for the occasion, came up to me and whispered, "Mrs. Ethridge, there is no meat."

It was ghastly, absolutely ghastly. I waked in a cold sweat. All those hungry people and no meat. I roused myself completely, sat straight up in the bed, and turned on the light. No meat . . . no meat . . . no meat. . . . What made the words so terrifying was that very next day, Sunday, Mark and I were having a luncheon for forty people. Thank God, not hundreds. Still, the thought of no meat for forty people was appalling.

But it couldn't be. The nightmare was only a nightmare. Calmly I went over in my mind the preparations for the party. As the weather was July hot, I had decided to have thinly sliced cold beef with fresh horseradish and sour cream sauce. Shug had kindly offered to cook it for me. So, on Friday morning, Mark and I had gone to the A & P and bought two large sirloin tips and carried them to Shug. Then, on Saturday morning, we had picked up the meat, carried it back to the A & P, and had it sliced by the accommodating butcher.

Then we had brought it back to The Land. At least I was pretty sure we had. I remembered getting to the checking counter and, having paid for the meat the day before, setting it to one side while we emptied out the basket of newly bought items.

Could we have left it on that checking counter? Did the boy who packed the bags leave out the meat? Of course not, I told myself.

So the nightmare was absurd. It meant nothing. Nothing! Reassured, I turned off the light, lay back down and went to sleep. And not once did I think of that meat again until the next day when, surrounded by chatting and drinking friends, I was approached by Mabel, who whispered in my ear, "Mrs. Ethridge, where is the meat?"

The meat! My heart fluttered frantically like a bird winged by a poor shot, then steadied somewhat. "In the refrigerator, of course," I whispered back.

"No ma'm; we've looked in the refrigerator already and it ain't there."

"Oh, dear, I must have absent-mindedly put it in the freezer."

"We done looked there too."

"Oh!" My heart began to flutter again—this time much more frantically—but I tried to appear calm so as not to alarm the guests. "Mabel, look again, please, and be thorough."

"Yes, ma'm," she said, and, with a shrug of her shoulders, left the room.

A few seconds later I followed her. I had to know the moment she and Lucille, who had arrived after her church service, found the meat. I could not stand the suspense. But when I reached the kitchen, they hadn't found it.

"Do you suppose I could have possibly in this hot weather left it in Mr. Ethridge's car?" I asked Lucille as she stood empty-handed in front of the refrigerator-freezer, her big, white-rimmed eyes popping out at me.

"I'm sure I can't answer that," she answered. "You know, Mrs. Ethridge, as well as I do you're liable to do anything."

There was no time for a rebuttal. "Mabel," I urged, "you go quickly and see if it's in Mr. Ethridge's car. It will give everybody ptomaine poison, but that's better than giving a luncheon with no meat."

The mention of ptomaine poison sent a fresh shudder through me. When Mark and I had had our first really big party on The Land, I had poisoned everybody except Bud and me. (I have, as the late Dr. Morris Flexner told me years ago, "buzzard blood.") I had prepared with my own hands beef stroganoff, using the freshest meat from the finest market in Chapel Hill and I had kept it refrigerated every minute; yet, just before dawn of the morning after the party I heard the toilets in Mark's and my bathroom and in the guest room where our dear friends, Mary San and Warwick Anderson, of Louisville, were staying being flushed frequently and furiously; but I thought nothing of it. Some people, especially Mark, have the habit of going to the bathroom very early; but when this rushing, roaring noise continued, I asked Mark if he was in some sort of trouble. Yes, he groaned, he was in terrible trouble. Still, I wasn't too alarmed, for Mark has always had a very delicate stomach; then, too, when Mary San and Warwick appeared for breakfast, they made light of their indisposition; it was really nothing, they insisted, though they barely touched their food.

It was not until afternoon that I learned I had absolutely shattered the morning service at St. Thomas's to which most of our guests belonged. Several members who had attended the party, including Shug, weren't able to make it to church at all; and those who did got up, one by one, looking ghastly wan and mildewy damp, and rushed for the door.

153 ॐ

Hearing these sickening facts from Bud, who had witnesesd this exodus, I went into the matter with two doctors and learned it was not the meat but more than likely the sour cream that had caused the diarrhea epidemic. They both said that every now and then sour cream "goes bad." I still don't understand it. I thought sour cream had already gone as "bad" as it could go. Still, I have never served beef stroganoff since.

Now, however, I was willing to serve any kind of meat. "Hurry, please Mabel. The guests are starving."

I stumbled to the back door to catch the first glimpse of Mabel returning from Mark's car, which was parked on the far side of the Social Circle. What was taking her so long? I wondered, about out of my mind. It couldn't take all this time to find the meat if it was there. And if it wasn't . . . ? I was unable to bring myself to face that possibility.

In another minute or two I saw Mabel, her long arms swinging weightlessly, coming along the winding path. With my heart thudding ever so heavily now, I hurried into the woods to meet her. "Where is the meat?" I panted.

"There wasn't any meat in the car."

"There has to be meat in the car," I insisted. "You didn't half look."

"Yes, ma'm, I did. I looked everywhere."

"Did you look in the trunk?" I demanded, though there was no earthly reason for the meat to be in the trunk; Mark and I had put all the groceries on the back seat.

"No'm."

"Come, hurry, we'll look in the trunk."

Fortunately Mark had left his keys in the car. We opened the trunk. There was no meat in sight. We dragged out the snow tires. Still no meat. We hauled out the wrench, the jack, the crocus sacks, the empty flower pots, the mildewed bathing suit. . . . Still no meat.

We started back across the Social Circle. Shug met us halfway. Through the front windows she had seen Mabel's exit from the kitchen door, followed closely by mine. Her first traumatic thought was that I had hurt her dear maid's feelings and had rushed out to apologize. "What's happened?" she called in alarmed tones.

I told her the situation as quietly as I could so as not to send her into hysterics; but then the horror of it got the better of me and I wailed, "Shug, you've got to do something! I really mean it, you've got to do something!"

"What do you want me to do—lay a cow right here in the middle of the Social Circle?"

I was in no mood for flippancy. By now I was seriously considering collapsing to the rocky, rooted ground in a deep coma and being carted off in an ambulance to the Memorial Hospital in Chapel Hill. That way the guests wouldn't even know there was no meat. They would just stand about in frightened, sympathetic groups, watching me depart; then quietly depart themselves.

However, I decided to postpone my collapse for a few more minutes in case a miracle happened. Returning to the kitchen, I begged Shug to find Bud. "I'm sure Bud can do something," I said.

Bud came. Quickly he made an inventory of the kitchen shelves: one can of salmon, one can of corned-beef hash, one jar of herring, two cans of clam soup, four cans of black bean soup. . . . The refrigerator was no better; eight eggs, one pound of bacon, a half role of sausage, a small triangle of every-day cheese. . . .

Glimpsing Mark making his unconcerned way by the kitchen door to the bar on the side porch, I flung myself in front of him and cried, "You've lost the meat! Do you hear me? You've lost the meat!"

What direction his dumfounded astonishment at this unjust accusation would have taken when he got his breath I can't say, for at that very moment Mabel appeared in the hall from out of a windowless coat closet, bearing in both hands the packages of sirloin. Evidently I, in my absent-minded way, finding, on our return from Sanford, the re-frigerator full of party food, had deposited the meat in this closet, knowing it to be practically unused in summer and amazingly cool from its air-conditioning unit.

But how did Mabel happen to look in there? She had seen me, she explained, put a watermelon in there the last time she had come to help prepare for a party.

The unanswered, spooky question, though, is why did I dream twelve full hours before this near catastrophe that it was going to happen?

20

Chatham County celebrated its bicentennial during June, 1971. The bicentennial committee, composed of practically everybody in the county who could either read or write, planned to have the celebration in January, since the county was actually formed on January 26, 1771, but somehow matters got delayed and the date had to be pushed back six months.

The county was named for William Pitt, the first Earl of Chatham, who, as a member of the English Parliament, fought for the rights of the Colonies, and Pittsboro was named for his son, William Pitt, the Younger, prime minister of England, though at the very beginning the town was called Chatham Court House. Pittsboro sprouts with iron plaques saying who lived where and when. Mark, a real history buff, can't pass one of these markers without slowing down to read it (it used to take us several days to get through Virginia on U.S. highway 1).

The bicentennial observance consisted of two main attractions: a tour of Pittsboro's historic sites and a week-long pageant; but for many weeks before the official celebration got under way, the people of the county were busy as a hive of bees sprucing up for the great days. The ancient, broken, heaved-up cement sidewalk of the one-block-long section of Hillsboro street was pried up and replaced by brick laid in sand, under the direction of my "dreaming" companion,

Mr. Le Clair, and most owners of stores on this main "drag" remodeled their many-colored, no-style fronts to resemble the Colonial shops of Williamsburg, Virginia.

Then, too, in spite of it being mid-summer, every Wednesday afternoon the women dressed in satins and brocades and ginghams with full, long skirts—trains, even!—dusting the ground and with high, boned collars and long, mutton sleeves; and the men who had them wore swallowtail coats and knee-length breeches and long white stockings and those who didn't own such finery donned open-necked, tieless shirts and blue jeans and sported long beards and hair.

Also a one-room slatted jail, nailed to the bed of a truck, parked on Hillsboro and the male citizens took turns behind the bars. The truck stuck so far into the street and the crowds gathered so enthusiastically about their locked-up friends that through traffic was no longer through. Mark and I avoided Pittsboro like the plague those Wednesday afternoons.

The first scheduled event, the tour, began on a sunny Sunday afternoon when the thermometer stood ("lay prone" is the more accurate phrase) at 92 degrees. Besides the old houses and public buildings of Pittsboro, it took in an antique water-run grist mill and a re-created old time blacksmith shop out in the country.

I had the pleasure of going on the tour with Mrs. Harry Horton, editor-in-chief of the bulky, just-off-the-press volume, *Chatham County 1771-1971*. At one point during the preparation of this historic work, Mrs. Horton reported that seventy-one people were writing chapters on subjects with which they felt they were especially conversant. Mark refused to accompany me, giving as his excuse the unusual heat; but I knew he believed he could learn more history from books without so much uncomfortable, physical exertion.

The tour started at the courthouse, a handsome, two-story pinkish-red brick building with large, creamy white columns across the front and a quaint wooden cupola on the roof. CHATHAM COUNTY, 1770 (the date the bill creating Chatham was introduced—it was not ratified until the following year) is embedded in the cement slab above the main entrance, but in truth it is the county's fourth courthouse and wasn't built until 1881.

Mark has never heard this disillusioning fact (I've carefully shielded him from it), so every time we have an out-of-town visitor, he drives him or her around the courthouse (it sits in a little park in the middle of Hillsboro Street) and points to the date with considerable pride.

Long before the cornerstone of this present courthouse was laid, or even before the cornerstone of the third courthouse was laid, it is alleged that a terrific storm, during the height of a trial, blew off the roof of the second courthouse and the terror and confusion were so great all the witnesses, jurors, court attendants, attorneys, and spectators stampeded out, leaving behind only the judge and the defendant. When order was finally restored, the judge directed the clerk to enter a verdict of "not guilty," proclaiming eloquently, "The defendant stayed by me when all others fled and now I will stand by him."

In front of the courthouse is the traditional bronze statue of a Confederate soldier. The figure is only seven feet tall, standing "at rest" on a granite shaft of twenty feet. With the granite base three times as tall as the statue and with the courthouse towering behind it, the figure appears quite diminutive, almost insignificant; but even so, its unveiling was, according to Mrs. Horton, one of the five outstanding events of Pittsboro's history in the hundred years since the Civil War, bringing the largest crowds the little town ever hosted. The other four events were: the celebration for the coming of the railroad, which has now disappeared except for a little spur that mostly hauls logs; the Shackleford hanging; the coming of electricity, when the people danced in the street; and the visit of Franklin D. Roosevelt. "Otherwise Pittsboro's existence," says Mrs. Horton understandably, "has been the routine day-to-day living of most small North Carolina towns."

Just getting the monument to Pittsboro was a "happening." It took five wagons, some of them drawn by four horses, and consumed two days, the men and animals having had to rest one night on the way in Bynum, to haul the monument the twenty-five miles or so from Durham where it was "made." And this was in August, 1907, just sixty-five years back.

Finally in place, more than four thousand people from all over the state came to see it unveiled. The occasion so inspired Edward L. Conn, writing in the September 20, 1962 edition of *The Chatham Record* issued to mark the 175th anniversary of the founding of Pittsboro, that he began his account with this fine flourish:

"The battle-scarred remnants of the gallant two thousand of Chatham's brave citizen soldiery who fought under the Southern Cross were assembled here today. . . ."

The Shackleford hanging brought even more people to Pittsboro than the unveiling of the monument or any of the other three top crowd-drawing events. It took place, so Mrs. Horton told me, on the slight rise called "Gallows Hill" in front of her house on Hillsboro Street, which I had seen many times and didn't need to visit this Sunday afternoon.

The account of the hanging was played up big in that

anniversary edition of the *Record*. A two-decker, eight-column headline of the blackest type across the top of the page declared: 5,000 PERSONS SWARMED INTO PITTSBORO ON MARCH 28, 1890 WHEN SHACKLEFORD DIED IN CHATHAM COUNTY'S LAST PUBLIC HANGING.

The "throngs" started coming the day before, the paper reported. "They came by covered wagon, by buggy, on horseback and some on foot. The night before the hanging campfires could be seen all over town."

The real name of the culprit wasn't Shackleford at all; it was James P. Davis, a fact the *Record* mentioned but didn't stop to explain. Evidently the writer was too carried away with the action to be bothered with such mundane information.

What had this Davis, alias Shackleford, done to meet such an end? To begin at the very beginning, the Justice of the Peace stated in an affadavit that on November 23, 1889, one J. W. Beavers came before him "and maketh oath that his brother-in-law, J. D. Horton, was found dead this morning buried in a tobacco barn" and he thought someone had "laid violent hands on him and taken his life and tried to conceal him."

After more details, the *Record* printed "in part" a bill of indictment, describing it as "a gem." The indictment accused James P. Davis, "having the fear of God before his eyes, but being moved and seduced by the instigation of the Devil," of "willfully and of malice aforethought" assaulting James D. Horton "with a certain hand axe at the value of six pence . . . and upon the top of the head did strike, penetrate and wound . . . giving one mortal wound of the length of three inches and of the depth of two inches. . . ."

The accused was quickly found guilty and sentenced to

be hanged "until he be dead on Gallows Hill." While waiting for the sentence to be carried out, Shackleford wrote a brief story of his life and, according to the *Record*, "it wasn't a pretty thing."

On the day of the hanging, the "execution procession" started out from the county jail behind the courthouse and proceeded up Hillsboro Street. The prisoner "was forced to ride to the gallows sitting on top of his wooden coffin and . . . he showed no trace of fear."

After Sheriff Brewer had sprung the trap, "scores of persons rushed toward the gallows to cut off bits of the rope to take home as good luck charms."

Turning our backs on the courthouse, where this most celebrated of Pittsboro's trials took place, Mrs. Horton and I strolled a block and a half down Hillsboro to the "Yellow House," dating back to 1787, making it the second house to be built in the county. (The oldest house burned some years back.) The "Yellow House" was built by an Irishman with the lovely name of Patrick St. Lawrence, who always wore flowing lace at his collars and cuffs and a carefully tended wig. But, alas, he came to a sad, sad pass. He lavished so much money on the house that he and the contractor went broke. He installed many expensive innovations, such as huge double doors from wall to wall and from floor to ceiling between the wide hall and two connecting parlors which could be lifted to the ceiling and fastened there when he and Mrs. St. Lawrence gave balls.

We were received at the front door by the present owners, Mr. and Mrs. Roddey Brower, who were dressed as elegantly as the St. Lawrences could ever have been, even to white powdered wigs from under which the perspiration rolled in rivulets. Many of their guests, especially the natives of Chatham, were attired in costumes too. Gingham sunbonnets bloomed all over the place.

One extremely tall, gaunt gentleman with a smut-dark, close-cut beard and dressed in a heavy black swallowtail coat and with a high silk hat, even in the house, looked so much like Abraham Lincoln, I ventured to say to him, "Sir, you are the spitting imagine of Mr. Lincoln."

"That's good to hear," said he, "for I am Mr. Lincoln."

"He means he plays the part of Abraham Lincoln in the pageant," Mrs. Horton quickly explained.

"I didn't know Abraham Lincoln came to Chatham County," I confessed.

"Oh, he didn't," said Mrs. Horton, "but the lady who wrote the pageant put Mr. Lincoln in it and nobody has been able to take him out, for the scene in which he appears is the most popular one in the whole pageant."

Mr. and Mrs. Brower had hoisted the big double doors to the ceiling as if they were having a ball and so I spent most of my time with head back and mouth open, studying the huge hooks in the ceiling and the rings in the doors to see just how the contractor had achieved this worthy innovation. If I had only known such a thing was possible, I would certainly have had such doors in our house, even if they had also broken dear Mark.

There were several other old homes on tour. As Mrs. Horton remarked, "It is amazing that there should be so many beautiful old homes when Pittsboro is so small—according to the census of 1960 it had only twelve hundred and fifty people and it hasn't grown any since—and also because in the first years of its existence there were so many fires. In fact, it had so many fires caused from the chimneys built of wood that the two aldermen passed an ordinance requiring only brick and mortar to be used. Yet here are these lovely homes from the past still standing."

That anniversary edition of *The Chatham Record* proclaims in headlines: ANCIENT PITTSBORO HAS MORE HISTORIC

RESIDENCES AND BUILDINGS STILL STANDING THAN ANY OTHER TOWN ITS SIZE IN STATE OF NORTH CAROLINA. Of course, that isn't claiming very much, considering the size of Pittsboro.

Chatham County's salubrious climate and location are given the credit for these handsome old dwellings. To escape the "miasmas" and humid heat of the coast, many of the wealthy rice planters from the coastal regions around Wilmington built summer homes in Pittsboro. Then, discovering that the winters were almost as pleasant as the summers, they decided to make it their permanent residence.

The miasma-free climate is due, so 'tis said, to the fact that the County is at the foot of what are referred to as the Unwharrie Mountains, but in truth look like hills. "They are worn down to the size of hills," Mrs. Horton told me, "because they are the oldest mountains in the United States." This remark struck me as amusing but, thank goodness, I didn't tell her so. Drawing on what Mark calls "my vast store of ignorance," I was under the impression that all mountains, oceans, and rivers were practically the same age. Evidently I couldn't have been more wrong. In the history, *Chatham County, 1771-1971,* the text says: "The Unwharrie Mountain Range, oldest range in the United States, has had a tremendous effect on the agriculture potential of the area involved. Erosion of these peaks from upward of 20,000 feet to 650 to 800 feet has taken away much of the natural top soil so that Chatham County has very little, if any, Class 1 soil in terms of agricultural capabilities." Well, now I know why we have only rocks on The Land. And all the time I had thought it was because we were on top of a bluff.

I didn't get to all these old houses; but I did visit the first brick building erected in Chatham at the cost of $1,350—the Presbyterian Church—and hear the joyful account of how its new steeple to replace the original, torn-down one had been raised just the past Thursday in the nick of time to have the bell, which had been brought from London in the early 1850's and for many years had no steeple in which to hang, installed and rung on this very auspicious Sunday morning.

We also went to the home of the Columbus Masonic Lodge, No. 102, constructed in 1838. We climbed the steep, winding stairs that led to the meetingroom on the second floor and were escorted about by a member of the lodge. Promptly my eyes were attracted to a large, full-length portrait of a gentleman I felt I had seen somewhere before, but couldn't place in these strange surroundings. Finally I asked the lodge member, "Please tell me whose portrait is that?"

"That," he answered, choked with shock, "is George Washington."

This was too much—both Abraham Lincoln and George Washington in one afternoon!

"Did George Washington sleep here too?" I questioned timidly.

"Not that I'm aware of," said the lodge member soberly, "but as you must know, George Washington was the first Grand Master of Masonry in America."

"No, I'm terribly sorry, but I didn't know."

I was chagrined, but not sufficiently to keep my big mouth shut. No sooner did I see what appeared to me to be a circle of electric lights, lighted, over a pulpit-like chair in which the presiding officer evidently sat to conduct the meetings of the lodge than I piped up again. "Sir, will you kindly tell me what that circle of lights is for?"

"That is not a circle; that's a capital G."

"Oh." For moment I held my tongue, but my curiosity was too much for me. "And what, sir, does the G stand for?"

"God."

"Oh."

We went to two more historic places, including the grist

mill and the blacksmith shop, but somehow the zest for sightseeing had gone out of me.

The Bicentennial Pageant played every evening for a week in Pittsboro's high-school football stadium. I wanted to go the very first evening when my friend, Mrs. Harry Horton, was to present Governor Bob Scott with a copy of *Chatham County, 1771-1971*, autographed by her and the other seventy writers, but Mark wouldn't budge. "I've seen a pageant," he said. However, toward the end of the week I wore him down and we went.

It was a warm, clear evening with the sun still high in the sky, which was too bad, for the pageant couldn't start until dark since a great portion of it was presented on slides. Yet the "curtain" hour was set for eight o'clock in order not to frighten the early-to-bed country people such as I with the suggestion of a late evening. The waiting, daylight hour was filled with slapstick comedy and very ordinary country music by a local group. I didn't dare steal even one little glance at Mark. I could feel him fuming, working up steam to escape. Mrs. Horton, who sat with us (she went every night) confessed to me later that she was even more nervous than I.

However, just in the nick of time, the pageant began and it moved fast and furiously. There were, of course, the events of two centuries to crowd into the evening. Since its foundation, Chatham had lived through the very stirring times of the Revolution and of the Tory raids; of the War Between the States, which had produced exceedingly noteworthy heroes, and of all the wars and years since.

Approximately four hundred people, both black and white and at least a hundred of them children, took part. Also there were horses, covered and uncovered wagons, buggies, cannons, rifles, campfires, log houses, and other paraphernalia. There were eleven long scenes, yet there was no change of scenery; just different areas of the mammoth stage were spotlighted for the different acts. People and horses trotted on and people and horses trotted off; campfires were lit, burned awhile and went out; rifles and cannon were shot and the smoke drifted away. It was truly spectacular, but only rarely did Mark and I have the slightest idea of what was happening. Just now and then could we hear what was being said. We thought the live choir of thirty or so men and women, who sang beautifully, enthusiastically, and almost continuously, were drowning the actors out, so we sat on the edge of our chairs, strained forward, and listened with all our might, only to learn afterward that the actors on the stage didn't speak. There were three or four readers in a booth somewhere far behind and above us giving forth all the lines over a loudspeaker.

Nevertheless, Mark and I enjoyed thoroughly the singing of the choir and I half expected Mark to join them at any moment.

The first time we heard a familiar name of a distinguished figure in Chatham's history and were able to fit the name to a figure appearing upon the stage was in Scene Nine, depicting the years of the Revolution. The name was that of the dashing, spendthrift Irishman, Patrick St. Lawrence, and the spotlight focused on a grand ball scene in the Yellow House. Couples were dancing the staid minuet and, according to the description that floated over the music from a reader, "the ladies are extravagantly attired and there are servants in abundance. The servants are black slaves."

Then we caught the name of General Cornwallis. I was particularly pleased to see the General. Though Mark, of course, had always been aware that General Cornwallis had played a significant role in North Carolina during the Revolutionary War, I had not known it until I moved to The Land. To be honest, I had never connected the General with any place in the United States other than Yorktown. He could have sprung just before that siege from the brow of an Indian maid on the shores of Virginia for all I knew. The fact is he actually slept in Chatham county; but also marched over a great part of the state. Amazingly, considering he did his very best to conquer the rebellious Tar Heels, his name is attached to streets, highways, and whole sections of North Carolina.

By the time of the pageant I had read considerably about him and had been anxiously waiting for him to appear. He had come to Chatham after the celebrated battle at Guilford Court House, now the city of Greensboro, which he won, but at terrific cost. (He said later, "I never saw such fighting since God made me. The Americans fought like demons.") The battle left him in a painful bind. His army was too mangled to fight again; but on the other hand, it was too dangerous for him to do nothing with his adversary General Nathanael Greene and the revolutionaries still in the area. Also, he had to have new men and supplies. He decided he must get in contact with the British fleet in Wilmington.

So he broke camp and started the slow, difficult march to the sea. The third day, he reached Chatham County. The army pitched its tents in an area now known as Cornwallis Heights (I told you whole sections were named for him) while the General stopped at the home of Major Mial Scurlock, who had recently died. He conducted himself, according to the report of Judge Walter D. Silver in that anniversary issue of *The Chatham Record*, "as a perfect British gentleman. . . . He treated Mrs. Scurlock and her children with great consideration, though she was outspoken in her devotion to American independence and was the widow of an officer of the State Militia and a mother of a soldier in the Continental Army."

Leaving the environs of Pittsboro, Cornwallis and his army stopped for several days at what was known in those times as Cornwallis's Ferry on Deep River, just a little way from where our Rocky flows into it, while they fashioned a pontoon bridge to get to the other side.

Though the citizens of North Carolina didn't realize it then, this long march of Cornwallis to the sea was the beginning of the end of The Revolution. When he finally reached Wilmington, he was still in a dilemma. Where to go next? He could march to Charleston, but that was where he had begun his expedition to conquer the Carolinas, or he could invade Virginia. Virginia appeared the preferable alternative, and that is where, as even I knew, he met his Yorktown. Surrounded by the French and American armies and by the French fleet, he surrendered to General Washington on October 19, 1781.

The second name we heard and recognized was that of David Fanning, the blackest Tory. Fanning, along with many other British sympathizers in this section, carried out a reign of terror. On July 16, 1781, he captured at one fell blow fifty-three citizens of Chatham, not to mention the courthouse itself. And a little later, on September 12, at Hillsboro, which was then the capital of the state, he captured the governor, Thomas Burke, and took him in chains to Charleston.

One historian, writing in that same special edition of *The Chatham Record,* waxed so wroth about Fanning he used up practically all the derogatory adjectives in the dictionary. "The Tory chieftain in this section, and the most successful, most daring and most cruel marauder of the state was David

Fanning," he declared. . . . "Upon the announcement of the War of the Revolution, he allied himself with the adherents of the British government and became a most active Tory. . . . He was engaged in many predatory adventures and soon acquired the reputation of being an unscrupulous, treacherous and inhuman partisan of the guerilla type. . . ." Otherwise he was, I presume, a good fellow.

All during the Revolutionary period, the chorus sang lustily: *America, Free America,* which was written, so I learned later, by Dr. Joseph Warren of Boston, the original Minute Man who "started Paul Revere off on his famous ride in 1775"; *Johnny Has Gone for a Soldier; Battle Cry of Freedom; What a Court Hath Old England;* and *Hail Columbia,* Washington's inaugural march.

The authors of the pageant, the director, the actors, the singers and the readers outdid themselves in Scene Ten, which was devoted to the War Between the States. Whole companies of soldiers in gray rushed to and fro; cannons roared, rifles popped; blood flowed; men died; and the chorus sang on.

Yet during this scene the voices of the readers rose above the bedlam of battle and the music and we heard: "Four hundred Chatham men gave their lives in that war, a war in which more Americans died than in all other wars combined—up to and including Vietnam."

I looked inquiringly at Mark, who knows everything, to see if this statement could possibly be true and he nodded his head, so it is so.

The reader continued: "While many of Chatham's men served gallantly in the Chatham Rifles, the Chatham Grays, the New River Boys and other companies, three Chatham natives made particularly notable contributions to 'The Cause.' "

Then we caught the name of John S. Lane, who "joined the Chatham Boys in Captain Billy Matthews' front yard and, moving from one battlefield to another, quickly rose to colonel of the 26th Regiment after the Battle of Gettysburg." At this moment, the Colonel rushed to the forefront of the battle, waving aloft the Stars and Bars. "Colonel Lane was the fourteenth man to seize the flag," a voice elaborated, "after twelve successive color bearers and Colonel Henry Burgwyn were shot down."

We saw the Colonel then "rush to the summit of the hill," the men in gray quickly following and the blue-clad Union fighters retreating into the darkness. But there was no time for rejoicing, for right at that moment Colonel Lane was shot in the neck and "the flag went down for the fourteenth time." A woman dashed out to stanch the wound and, though it seemed incongruous to see her there in the tumult of battle, it was well she did, for the Colonel "survived the wound" and "achieved the highest rank of any Chathamite in the Confederate Army."

We also heard the name of Henry A. London, "who along with the entire senior class left the University of North Carolina in 1864," but whether Private London was among the coming-and-going heroes on the stage I could never tell. However, I did make out from the loudspeaker that he distinguished himself by carrying General Robert E. Lee's last order at Appomattox in April, 1865—the order to cease fire.

Next, the name of Captain James Iredell Waddell boomed forth. We were familiar with it too, for much has been written about the captain. We didn't even have to try to hear what the voice was proclaiming above the choir's rendition of the song, *Shenandoah*. During the war, this gallant Southerner was captain of the clipper, the *Shenandoah*. She had been a British clipper, the *Sea King*, but was transferred to the Confederacy through intrigue as sly as any seen on television today. However, I won't go into it at this late date, except to say the plot was concocted by James D. Bullock, naval agent and chief of the Confederate Secret Service Abroad and, incidentally, the uncle of Theodore Roosevelt.

The *Shenandoah* was considered the greatest prize. She was 222 feet long and weighed 1,160 tons. She could cruise either by sail or steam and was built to transport troops and tea.

For the next six months Captain Waddell sailed the *Shenandoah* around the world, hunting Union shipping in every sea except the Antarctic. And the hunting was very good. He captured thirty-eight ships, destroying thirty-two of them and releasing six on bond, and taking 1,053 prisoners. The captured vessels were valued at more than $1,200,000.

But it wasn't these prizes that won for Captain Waddell his memorable niche in Confederate history. It was his belated surrender of the *Shenandoah* six months after the war was officially ended at Appomattox. According to his own memoirs he didn't get the news of the end of the conflict because of the waters in which he was pirating—the North Pacific between Alaska and Russia, thirteen days out of San Francisco. This fact was in the original manuscript of the pageant, Mrs. Horton told me, but was cut out. And though she didn't tell me why it was omitted, I strongly suspect it was because Chathamites don't care for that version of their hero's surrender; they much prefer to believe the intrepid captain continued his pirating in spite of being fully aware of the Confederacy's capitulation.

Shortly after the recitation of the captain's feats, the scene of the War Between the States drew to a close with the appearance of my old friend of Sunday afternoon portraying

Abraham Lincoln. I recognized him right off. He drove onto the stage in a sad-looking, sagging buggy with a black top—but no fringe. He had come to declare that the bitter struggle was over and that all the people of the United States should live in friendship and peace. The choir spiritedly sang *The Battle Hymn of the Republic*.

After this was a long scene of modern times during which the choir gave forth among other numbers some of Mark's favorite pieces: *In the Evening by the Moonlight; I've Been Working on the Railroad; Carolina in the Morning; In the Good Old Summertime;* and *God Bless America*. During these renditions, I kept a firm hold on his arm and murmured, "Down, boy."

Driving home, Mark and I were full of admiration for the people of our adopted county, who had so many colorful, heroic figures in their background and had the talent and stamina to bring them back to life.

21

Our years in North Carolina up to this writing climaxed one August when all the children and grandchildren, except Bubber and his wife Peg and their four; and Marc, the husband of Georgia; and Mr. Big; and Sefton, the thirteen-year-old of Shug and Bud, who was away at camp, gathered on The Land to revel in just being together and, as I'm fond of saying, "to keep love going on."

There were Shug and Bud and their two, Mark A. and Georgia Snow; Big Georgia and her four: David, Jenny, Georgia Cubbedge, and Mary Howell; and Eleanor and her three: David, Nathaniel, and Mark V. We had wall-to-wall sleeping bags in the living room and on the side porch.

For the first week the visit of Eleanor and the little boys caused the greatest excitement, for we had not seen them for a year. We enjoyed their visit, I'm afraid, more than they did, for David and Nathaniel had traumatic experiences I should have expected and taken in my stride since I was familiar with their accident-prone history, but I have a talent for wiping past calamities quickly from my mind. So I was terribly shaken up one afternoon when blood-curdling screams split the air for miles around. Scream after scream. Wild, full-bodied, huge-lunged screams. Caruso at the height of his career couldn't have approached them. They were exploding from the throat of little David, then eight. He had stumbled into a colony of wasps, and had been stung on every exposed part of his body. And a lot of it was exposed, for he had on only minute bathing shorts, as he was on the way to the river to bob over the rapids on the inner tube of an automobile tire.

For an hour, while he screamed and screamed without a second's letup, Eleanor, Big Georgia, Jenny and I applied cubes of ice, moving them frantically from one sting to another, and plastered him with baking soda and dosed him with aspirin. He wasn't allergic, thank God, to wasp stings; he was just extremely sensitive to the excruciating pain they wrought and didn't give a damn who knew it. No woman in childbirth ever yelled louder and longer.

Finally, when all four of us first-aiders were exhausted and he showed no signs of letting up, we persuaded him to jump in the garden pool and submerge himself under its icy-cold water. I, for one, didn't even look to see if he ever surfaced.

By the next morning he was practically recovered; but there was no time to relax. Nathaniel, aged five, wallowed, so it seemed, stark naked in a patch of poison ivy, undiscovered until that moment, and developed sheets of tiny, steaming, itching blisters from the base of his skull to the soles of his feet. He writhed and wailed one whole night, in spite of the salve we applied. If that long-suffering emergency room in Chapel Hill hadn't been twenty-two miles away, we would certainly have had him in it.

But, excepting those two painful "happenings," the days were full and joyous, especially the day my brother, Wim, chartered a plane and flew Mother, ninety-nine years and four months old, along with the wheelchair she had been obliged to use since she broke her hip three years before, and two of his grandchildren, Bill and Katherine, from Macon to Sanford to spend five hours with us. Mother's coming was a complete surprise. Wim had told us that he and the children were coming and Mark had gone to the airport to meet them; but he hadn't mentioned Mother. He evidently wanted to see Shug, who is very emotional, and me burst into tears of shock and ecstasy.

For an hour or more Mother, sitting on the deck to drink in the view, entertained the eleven great-grandchildren with quick, bright answers to their questions and lighthearted teasing. She insisted she was not ninety-nine, which didn't surprise us grownups, for she had always insisted she was younger than her father's handwriting in the big family Bible says—she was "only ninety-seven." It was a dastardly plot of her children, said she, to make her older than she was. When we reminded her of all the birthdays we had celebrated in a big way, beginning with the ninetieth, when the mayor of Macon gave her the key to the city (which she promptly told him she didn't need for she could go anywhere she pleased, including the jail, without it), she simply shrugged and made faces at us. Her longevity, be it ninety-seven or ninety-nine, she attributes to "God first and water second."

On being told of Nathaniel's bout with poison ivy, she recalled the long-ago-time in Kentucky when she had put Mr. Big, only a year or so old and completely naked, for he was taking a sunbath, on a lush vine she had tugged out of a pink dogwood and pulled him about the lawn, only to realize that night as he writhed in pain that the vine had been poison ivy.

I, of course, remembered it too and I also remembered the indignant speech she had made the next morning. Standing in the middle of the library, her little yellow-green eyes flashing, she had proclaimed: "I knew Kentucky was a wicked state; I knew Kentucky manufactured cigarettes; I knew Kentucky made whisky; I knew Kentucky had horse races; but I didn't know Kentucky had poison ivy."

After the bantering and reminiscing session, she played the piano for forty-five minutes for everybody to sing. With her beautiful, deeply wrinkled face flushed as pink as the pinkest carnation with exhilaration and her snow-white, curly-haired head nodding in time to the music, she played *Little Brown Jug; I Wish I Were Single Again; Whispering Hope; Abide with Me; What a Friend We Have in Jesus; When the Roll Is Called Up Yonder,* and other familiar Baptist hymns. She played lustily, with all her strength, and she sang so hard in her once rich, but now thin, alto voice that the veins stood out on her neck.

(It took me back to the days when she had sung her heart out at church and at the prayer meetings she had conducted for the Negroes in the alley behind our house in Macon. One occasion was especially vivid. A Negro baby had been born blue before sunup on a hot, July day and had died around noon. Piercing wails swept skyward.

"Pra-ise de Lawd," high, thin sopranos wailed. "Pra-ise de Lawd. He give and He take away. Pra-ise de Lawd."

"Pra-ise de Lawd. May He take me," pleading tenors cried. "Pra-ise de Lawd. May He take me."

Mother's nerves finally shattered. She marched to the alley, I following timidly at her heels. She went directly to the shack where the blue baby lay and addressed herself to the mourners gathered there.

"Why keep begging the Lord to take you?" she demanded. "Do you want to die?"

"No'm, but when we does, we want de Lord to take us," one woman answered.

"But you are asking the Lord to take you. If the Lord

answers your prayers, you'll be dead Negroes tomorrow. I think you had better hush immediately."

They stared at her, shocked, eyes stretched wide.

"The thing for you to do is to go about your business and leave the Lord to attend to His."

After that, the afternoon was very still and quiet and when evening came, the melancholy was so deep Mother was troubled by it. "I think I will go in the alley and have a prayer meeting," she said. "A prayer meeting will cheer everybody up."

Gathering up her Bible and a half dozen hymn books, she went out and soon the night rang with "Throw out the life line . . . . throw out the life line. . . . Someone is sinking today. . . ."

Throw Out the Life Line was followed by *Jesus, Lover of My Soul*, and then there was silence. I thought Mother must be praying, but when the silence continued, I was puzzled. Then Mother came in, her cheeks red and her eyes snapping. A young Negro woman had broken up the prayer meeting. She had slipped out of her house and gone to the home of her landlady on Arlington Street and complained that the hymn-singing was disturbing her rest.

The landlady hurried to the alley and relayed the complaint to Mother, who was her friend. Mother turned to the Negro woman. "Now, just why do you object to our singing?"

"Hymn-singing does sumpin' to me inside," she answered.

"That is the spirit moving you!" Mother cried exultantly.

"That is jes' what I'm scared of. . . . I don't want no spirit moving me.")

At dinner, which we had at two o'clock with seventeen sitting down at two tables, Mother said the blessing with a few extra remarks of gratitude and beneficial requests for her children, grandchildren, and "greats" who were "gathered around this board," then settled down, so we all thought, to eating.

She had always had an excellent appetite; in fact, she frequently described herself as a "general eater" and was eager to begin every meal. She actually got a bit impatient if she had to wait more than a couple of minutes after a meal was announced. Once, when visiting us at Prospect at the same time Shug and Bud were staying with us, right after the birth of Sefton, she fumed about Bud not coming to the table promptly. "Bud," she said with considerable asperity, "is seemingly indifferent to food until he gets to the table."

She usually ate everything on her plate and ended up, no matter what had gone before, with a sweet. The richer, the better. Well aware of this weakness of hers, Mark, on one occasion when she was in her late nineties and we took her to a restaurant for dinner, ordered the most expensive dessert on the menu, which arrived looking like a miniature Eiffel Tower—a thick layer of chocolate cake, a huge dip of vanilla ice cream, and on the top of the ice cream a big blob of whipped cream centered with a cherry. Instantly Mother shouted, "Bingo!"

However, this reunion day she didn't "dig in." Instead, after a few minutes, she abruptly announced: "I'm moving. I won't sit here by Mark and be tormented another minute." And with that she backed her wheelchair from the table with amazing expertise for one approaching a hundred.

"I'm sorry, Mrs. Snow," said Mark. "I didn't mean to torment you."

"Your apology comes too late," retorted Mother and maneuvered herself farther down the table, several people shifting to make room for her.

Among shouts of laughter, dear, embarrassed Mark, whom Mother has always loved dearly, tried to explain that all he had done was to say several times, "Eat, Mrs. Snow. Go ahead and eat," when she seemed inclined to dawdle over her food; but evidently he said it once too often.

In the afternoon, Mother, Wim, the two grandchildren, and Jim Lowe, the pilot, drove to the Sanford airport to fly back to Macon. Bud, Mark A., and I went along to see them off. It was a little six-seater plane, sitting, so it appeared to me, mighty high off the ground. I didn't see how my ancient Mother could possibly get in it, especially since there were no steps, or even a ladder.

While Jim Lowe was filing his flight plan, Mark A. managed to climb up on the wing and stick his head in the plane and look about. As he withdrew his head and was standing rather precariously on the wing, Wim swooped Mother up in his arms and, with Bud's help, hoisted her up to him. Startled out of his wits, Mark A. demanded, "What? . . . What? . . ."

"Take her and put her in the plane," said Wim.

Mark A., looking as if he might faint any moment, clutched Mother's frail body to him, staggered to the door that opened off the wing, struggled through it, and deposited Mother in the seat behind the pilot's.

A few minutes later they were off. As they winged by us, the wheels just clearing the ground, we spied Mother, smiling and waving her handkerchief vigorously against the window, as had always been her custom on leaving us.

A courageous woman, my mother. I just hope when my time comes to say a final good-by to this beautiful life I've had by the side of Mark, I can smile and wave my handkerchief half so gallantly.